New Humanities and Academic Disciplines

New Humanities and Academic Disciplines
The Case of Jewish Studies

Edited by

Jacob Neusner

Wipf & Stock
PUBLISHERS
Eugene, Oregon

Wipf and Stock Publishers
199 W 8th Ave, Suite 3
Eugene, OR 97401

New Humanities and Academic Disciplines
The Case of Jewish Studies
By Neusner, Jacob
Copyright©1984 by Neusner, Jacob
ISBN: 1-59244-953-0
Publication date 10/18/2004
Previously published by The University of Wisconsin Press, 1984

For my comrades, in bad times and good, *Wendell S. Dietrich and Ernest S. Frerichs,* in celebration of our founding of Brown University's Program in Judaic Studies, 28 February 1981–12 August 1982

Contents

Introduction: From Yeshiva to University   ix

Part One: The Academic Study of Judaism

    1. Modes of Jewish Studies in the University   3

      Jacob Neusner
      Brown University

Part Two: Academic Disciplines and Jewish Learning

    2. Here and Now: Prospects for Graduate Education   33

      Jonathan Z. Smith
      University of Chicago

    3. Judaism within the Disciplines of Religious Studies: Perspectives on Graduate Education   46

      Jacob Neusner
      Brown University

    4. Contemporary Jewish Studies in the Social Sciences: Analytic Themes and Doctoral Studies   62

      Calvin Goldscheider
      Hebrew University and Brown University
      Alan S. Zuckerman
      Brown University

    5. Graduate Training in Hebrew Literature   79

      Robert Alter
      University of California, Berkeley

6. Graduate Education in Modern Hebrew
   Literature   95

   Arnold J. Band
   University of California, Los Angeles

7. The Role of Language in Graduate Programs of
   Jewish Studies   106

   Baruch A. Levine
   New York University

8. Graduate Education in Jewish Philosophy   121

   Marvin Fox
   Brandeis University

9. Graduate Studies in Jewish History   135

   Marc Lee Raphael
   Ohio State University

Part Three: Other Possibilities

10. The Three Academic Cultures of Graduate
    Education in Jewish Studies   153

    Ivan G. Marcus
    Jewish Theological Seminary of America

Part Four: The Larger Context

11. Jewish Studies and the New Humanities   167

    Jacob Neusner
    Brown University

Acknowledgments   181

Index   183

Introduction

From Yeshiva to University

Certain things we know and hold to be facts. We take it for granted that any objective, or at least reasonable, person will concede their truth. And the ways we know those facts—acquire them, think about them, make use of them, and build new facts or structures of meaning upon them—we presume are equally obvious. Whether the proposition is that one and one add up to two, or that every American should know the history of America, the claim is the same. We think the reason needs no spelling out.

Nothing could be further from the truth. We know only what we are taught. We are taught what people value and so have decided we should be taught. We acquire that small part of the wisdom accumulated by humanity, because we are born into a given family, community, state, nation—here, not elsewhere. The things we know come to us from the family and society that nurture us. We know those things because they are useful in the setting of our lives. Their importance derives, in the end, from decisions made by others, long ago and far away. For instance, that numbers should run in groups of ten, rather than six or twelve, or that things that happen in the world may be worth retelling and studying, represent decisions someone made. So nothing is a given. No fact is a datum of some reality "out there." No knowledge stands independent of context and culture, self-evidently true and worth knowing as much to us Americans as to the Hottentots, the Papuans, or the Ainu of Hokkaido.

It follows that each society accumulates facts and selects among them those worth handing on. Each community develops modes of answering questions deemed worth asking. Each culture determines that this is the right way, and that is the wrong way, to think through a problem and identify its proper solution. Just as there are many kinds, or systems, of mathematics, each with its own generative propositions, so there are many systems of learning, each with its givens, its conventional ways of thinking about established and perennial questions, its self-evident truths and its unthinkable thoughts.

What makes the history and sociology of learning interesting is not merely the diversity of traditions of learning. Changes in the curriculum of a school or the contents of a set-piece examination over time serve as indicators of culture, barometers of the life of the community. Still more indicative of what is happening in politics and society is the way in which, through one kind of institution rather than another, a given culture determines to transmit knowledge, on the one side, and produce new knowledge, on the other. So the institutional settings for learning—who has power to decide who teaches what to whom, and with what consequences for the life and career of the one who learns—govern the shape and uses of knowledge.

Even within the university setting, we tend to obscure the extraordinary differences among the remarkably various institutions in which young people, from eighteen to twenty-two years of age, spend their time in the status of what we call "students." Just as not all students are like one another, with some spending their time reading books or conducting experiments or playing sports, and others spending their time in a way we would perhaps call "wasteful," so under the flag of a college or a university sail many strange vessels indeed. Some are rowboats, some are battleships (and just as obsolete).

Accordingly, if we travel to another society and attempt to have a conversation about education with the aid of a dictionary, we discover that our dictionary misleads us. True, for "school" we learn that there is *école*, or *Gymnasium*, or *university*, or *institute*. But all these things are not the same, although they may turn out to point toward what is in the end the same thing. Once we recognize the diversity of meanings associated with "learning" and "institutions of learning," we confront yet another disorderly fact. In our own society, the institutions we regard as permanent, as givens of our culture, come out of a strikingly short history indeed. They are the outcome not of a millennium but of less than a century. Colleges and univer-

Introduction

sities in America before the twentieth century bear slight resemblance to the ones we now know, even if, in some instances, they bear the same name. The cow college becomes the great center of research. The tight little island for the privileged few turns into a center of learning for remarkably diverse young people, each with his or her own aspiration. And the path of history is not always onward and upward; great universities decay, especially when, with perfect faith, they believe their own press releases.

It follows that, if we want to understand what is happening to people, we do well by reflecting upon what is happening to traditions of learning and to the institutions of learning. The things we know, the places in which we learn them, the value attached to knowing one thing rather than some other, the convention of knowing one thing in some way, rather than in some other way—these tell us what is going on in the great world beyond the mind. Lest we think the issues trivial, we have only to consider the weight religious traditions and political systems attach to schooling. In our own country, we expect the schools to provide a solution for all our social dilemmas. So institutions of learning become agents of social change. That is how it should be: learning and the way learning is defined and transmitted really do define who we are and what we shall become. So it is right that the schools should be the battlefield of culture: it is the tribute of society to schools. If books can be burned, it is because they pose dangers to people with the strength to light a match, the conscience to kindle the flame. Accordingly, when we study what is happening in traditions of learning, we approach the most profound issues of social and cultural change.

This book is about social change as it is even now being revealed in the creation of a new field of learning, in an unprecedented setting, and for an as-yet-unknown cultural and intellectual purpose. It is about how a field of learning moves from one kind of institution to another, is practiced by new people (women, not only men, and outsiders as well as insiders), and for new purposes (secular, not only religious) and in new ways. Out of these minute particulars, in our imagination we may reconstruct the whole of modern history—the universe out of a grain of sand.

Perhaps no group in the past two hundred years of revolutionary change has moved so far, so fast, and in so many directions as the

Jews. Nearly universally despised as the dregs of society, incapable of idealism, of serving a country, fighting in an army, or organizing a government, in a mere fifty years the Jews built a state. Within another handful of decades, they established a tradition of military valor admired even by their enemies. Wholly enveloped in a parochial culture, speaking a language others heard as jargon, perceived by the world at large as lacking all traits of worthwhile education, within three generations in Western Europe, and still more rapidly in America, the Jews passed into the upper layers of cultural life, making whole professions and fields of science and learning nearly their own. In 1900 nearly all Jews in the world lived in Eastern Europe. Eighty years later, half the Jews in the world lived in America, a quarter in a Jewish state, the State of Israel, and the rest in Western countries. In 1900 people commonly supposed Jews could not go into mathematics or physics. They were thought to have no innate gifts for those fields. Albert Einstein was even then at work. Jews in America and the USSR played critical roles in making nuclear energy a reality in war and peace. So the point is clear. But one aspect of it is not.

In all of these vast and profound changes, as the Jews moved from one language to another, from one system of politics to another, from one place to another, and from one world view to another, what happened to their particular traditions of learning? For the Jews had nurtured a system of learning, a tradition of what to study and how to study, for a continuous history of nearly two thousand years. That learning until our own day focused principally on sacred literature, called "Torah," meaning divine revelation. This literature encompassed the Hebrew scriptures ("the Old Testament"); the Mishnah, a late-second-century code of laws; the Babylonian and Palestinian Talmuds, expansions and extensions of the Mishnah; as well as various codes, commentaries, and other secondary developments of the laws; and compositions of exegeses of scripture called *midrashim*. So "Torah" began with scripture and the Mishnah. Everything else was so composed as to serve as commentary to those two documents. In the nineteenth century, in the first great revolution in Jewish learning, these topics were joined in German Jewish scholarship by extensive work in three others: Jewish philosophy, Jewish poetry and other literature (both the works of the Middle Ages), and Jewish history,

Introduction

covering all periods in a rather conservative way. The great innovations in critical historiography of the age made only a slight impact. These Jewish historians collected and arranged stories and then retold them in their own words. Still, the expansion of the curriculum, in Western Europe and America, in its day signified the reform of Judaism. For a hundred years, Jewish learning in the Western, modern mode owed nearly all of its principal traits to the decision of Reform Jews and their near-at-hand opponents. It was, then, Reform and Conservative Judaism in the study and Jewish academy that reshaped learning as they reformed the old Judaism.

The classical curriculum had always been studied in *yeshivot*. Through processes of repetition and memorization of the text as the teacher said it, then ritualized questions and conventional answers, the work went forward. Brilliance lay in finding ever more acute distinctions. A great deal of hand wagging and shouting signified commitment to the process. Enormous erudition won recognition even for the superior human merits of the learned man (no women were involved until our own day). Status came from the approbation of the elders. Solid achievement in the form of the writing of articles and books stood for little and was actively discouraged. Yet the outcome was creative: the definition of a whole civilization of Israel, the Jewish people. The culture of the Jews emerged, deeply devoted to a classical text, profoundly shaped by the viewpoints of that text and those who knew it. The Yiddish-speaking Jewish nation in Poland, Russia, Rumania, and surrounding lands framed and formed its culture in the pages of classical rabbinic texts. These defined the ethos of the nation and the ethics of everyday life. If we can imagine a storekeeper or common laborer invoking a saying out of Milton or Shakespeare for every situation in life, we can begin to understand what it meant for a whole world to spring forth from a book.

Who studied in *yeshivot*? Only Jewish males, as I said. Who taught? Only people whose entire education had taken place in *yeshivot* and under the guidance of the old masters of the day. What happened to the student? He returned home and made a living as best he could. Education bore no relationship to earnings. The disciple's education in the Talmud and related sciences in no way advanced his career, except in a spiritual sense, on the one side, and in that social range in which learning won honor, on the other. The educational system, bottom to top, was one and integrated, from the beginning in a small room in which youngsters memorized the alphabet and the prayers, to the climax in the vast hall of a *yeshiva,* marked by the yelps and shouts of vigorous argument. There were no degrees in any sense known to us. True, people might learn the rules of various ritual functions and so master various religious specialties. But the ideal was that of the amateur in the most noble sense: learning for the sanctity of what was learned, learning to come to climax in holy deeds, learning what God had told Israel, the Jewish nation—learning in the service of God.

So among the treasures of incalculable value coming down to us from the minds of antiquity—the philosophy of Socrates, Plato, and Aristotle, the Hebrew scriptures, the New Testament, the law and politics of Rome, for instance—none has served so long to sustain the very society that originally nurtured it as has the system of learning of Judaism. If the four-hundred-year-old Protestant tradition of Bible study were to continue for another fifteen centuries, until A.D. 3500, it would only begin to approach the longevity enjoyed by the sacred sciences of Judaism. If American Protestants during those millennia were to be scattered among a hundred countries and to speak a hundred languages other than American English, but were to continue to study the Bible in the King James translation and with the American-language commentaries of Luther or Calvin wherever they went; and if, some two thousand years from now, the Southern Presbyterians of Peru were to return to America, speaking Quechua but still studying in our American language the classics of the faith and culture of American Protestant life; and if they then were to found America again, as it had been twenty centuries before; and if, when America reborn came to life, they were to teach in the schools the American language they had preserved for twenty centuries, the holy books they had sustained and been sustained by—if they did all this, then, but only then, we should find an approximate analogy to the amazing record at hand. This is what is at issue when we ask: And today, what of "Torah"? And what of Talmud? And what happens now to Jewish learning? At issue are facts produced by this most remarkable saga in the history of human culture.

Yet the analogy is still not quite adequate. For the Jews in modern times have not only preserved their old books, to be read in the old

Introduction

ways in institutions—*yeshivot*—claiming to replicate in all countries the classical patterns of life and learning in the old country. Jewish intellectuals and scholars of Judaism, now joined by non-Jews, have also been creating in a wholly new setting, namely, the university, a completely fresh way of studying their holy books, on the one side, and a totally unprecedented choice of what is studied as "Jewish learning," on the other. So old things are learned in new ways. Things never before studied now fall into the category of the old things, that is, of Jewish learning. A completely fresh set of questions is addressed to both the old and the new—all in all, amazing.

We should expect that, as people responded to social change by learning new things, they also would cease to pursue the old and no-longer-relevant sacred sciences. To be sure, the many who rejected modernization remained within the ancient learned disciplines as well. But the still larger part of Jewry that made the move to modernity took with them intellectual traditions they might have left behind. They reshaped the old modes of learning to accommodate the new setting. That is the amazing fact recorded (if not celebrated) in this book.

So the established intellectual tradition of the Jews moved in a way not to be predicted. It endured but experienced Westernization. It was a move made possible by the very character of Western, and, in particular, American, culture. What happened is something for which, I think, we can find not a single analogy in the history of human knowledge: *America made room for Jewish learning in the institutions of American education and scholarship.* And some Americans, not of Jewish origin, undertook to add to their education the things to be learned from the experience and wisdom of the Jewish people, as these might be studied in books, in university classrooms. There is no precedent, no imaginable counterpart, in all of the history of the Jewish people. The unprecedented opportunity available to Jewish learning proved part of a larger cultural vision of America, itself exceptional in history. Just as America received diverse peoples, so its diverse peoples, forming one nation, determined to receive and grant a hearing to diverse traditions of learning. That is why, in American universities, we can study a far greater range of the social cultures of humanity than can be imagined in any other university system.

American universities now turn out to be "second-best" to all other universities in the world in the study of all other cultures. Let me clarify this odd point. The best place to learn Hebrew language and literature is in the universities of the State of Israel. The second best places in all the world are in the University of California and in New York University (to give two instances of exceptionally distinguished centers for the study of Hebrew, as the participants in this book demonstrate). But the same is so of German and French, of British history and Byzantine art. And, if truth be told, there are some things we might do better than the natives.

So the fact is that in today's universities aspects of Jewish sacred sciences come under study which rarely before have been studied by non-Jews, in schools created for neutral purposes and sponsored by non-Jews.

In this there is something paradoxical. What defined what was special and different about the intellectual life of the Jews? It is what they learned in their holy books. The sight of a gentile studying Talmud is as surprising as it would be to see an elephant dance, or a chicken lecture on atomic physics. It amounts to the absurd: the utter confusion of categories and classifications. But it is not at all absurd any more.

But, of still greater consequence, whatever pertains to the Jews today forms a legitimate and routinely accepted subject of study, whether the subject is old or new. And that is with little precedent. True, the Inquisition took an interest in Judaism, and so have occasional preachers and missionaries. But these form no exception to the rule that, before now, Jewish learning served Jewish purposes, defined and carried out by Jews as teachers, Jews as students, Jews as sponsors of the institutions of learning, Jews as beneficiaries of the entire enterprise of the Jewish intellect. Not only the sacred sciences, but all of the things one might want to know about any group, today define the list of things in which courses about the Jews take shape.

In attempting to describe and explain how this unprecedented event in the history of learning even now is taking place, in this book I have selected only one point of entry, one small aspect of the much larger phenomenon at hand. At issue is a topic not apt at first glance to address critical issues urgent for a broad audience, namely, how

Introduction

various scholarly disciplines absorb and reshape diverse areas of Jewish learning, specifically, in the setting of graduate education. What an unimaginably small subject! But in selecting it, I chose the moment in the formation and transmission of a tradition of learning at which everything is held in suspense, all decisions made afresh, so to speak. Graduate school is the moment at which a student becomes a teacher, and an authority is born for the coming generations. Graduate education turns the amateur into a professional. Properly conducted, it provides that experience of the coming professional years that transforms a learned young person into a professor—the experience of socialization to the profession. Graduate education, to be sure, also provides lessons. Graduate schools not only change people. They teach things. They not only prepare people to qualify for jobs. They also provide students with things to teach when they get jobs as professors. So in graduate school we make those decisions that shape the field of the future. We determine how to shape the mind and intellect of our society for generations to come. And, it should be said, since most (though by no means all) important scholarship in the humanities emerges from professors who also are teachers of doctoral students, the ideas people will hold as self-evident a hundred years from now today emerge in just this setting, from just these people in this kind of institution. Here the future is born—and we in this book decide what it will look like in one detail.

Now let me briefly account for the title of this book and for the character of the papers. What do I mean by "academic disciplines"? To state matters very simply, by "discipline" I mean the way we frame our questions. It is how we define what we want to know *about* a given subject, on the one side, and how we go about answering those questions, testing the answers, and using the results for further inquiry, on the other. The distinguishing characteristic of Western, secular learning derives from its self-consciousness about matters of method. That is its power to articulate not only what we know but how we find it out and why we think it is worth knowing. So we not only know something. We realize how we know it: because we asked a given kind of question and so paid attention to a certain sort of information, rather than some other. That realization lies at the foundation of learning. It is what we teach in graduate school, when we turn a learned student into a scholar of independent capacities of mind.

The way in which Jewish learning, in particular, has been organized focuses upon quite other matters than disciplinary ones. The departments of a Jewish seminary, for instance, tend to bear the titles of books, not of disciplines: department of *Bible,* department of *Talmud.* Yeshivot, for their part, regard as useless the sort of specialization, and even differentiation, represented by departmental organization of subjects even by book titles. Their noble ideal is of a pious man of broad learning, knowledgeable in a vast area of useful knowledge, ignorant only of things not worth knowing. To that cultural ideal, the notion of differentiation of things of learning is alien. All differentiation—picking and choosing what to know and how to know it—takes place, so to speak, at the gates of the schoolhouse. What is inside by definition is worth knowing. What is outside is not worth knowing. We may draw an analogy to the Soviet approach to studying the phenomena of religion—in institutes of the study of religion *and atheism.*

Let me expand on this point, since it is suggestive beyond itself. In *yeshivot,* everything that is learned is learned in the same way. Of course, everything is equally worth knowing. Everything that is ignored is deliberately ignored: all things equally *not* worth knowing. So there are only two departments: the department of Torah, the department of everything else—everything worthless. Everything that falls into the classification of Torah is equally Torah. That is the foundation of the system.

When Jewish seminaries, organized as institutions of the West, resort to the mode of organization familiar from universities, they borrow the language; hence, "department of. . . ." But they do not understand, and cannot fully make use of, what the language stands for. A university department, program, or center not only studies a given topic. It studies a topic in a well-defined way. A department of French studies not the wine production in the Loire but the literature and language of France. A department of sociology or economics deals with specific things—race relations or velocity of money. But it does so in accord with a discipline present, under ordinary circumstances, wherever and whenever any given, specific thing comes under study. The *how* is the same: the *what* alone shifts. That is why

Introduction

a student in a sequence of courses in a given department may move from one topic to the next, while what the student *does* in learning about a sequence of diverse topics remains one and the same. What happens in universities, with their stress on method, therefore, is that the particular is forced to serve as an exemplification of the general. What is specific turns outward to address issues of general concern. What is private becomes public. What is arcane gains intelligibility. That is what we mean by a university, a place in which we speak of universals, asking the same thing about everything. All of this we encompass within two words, (1) "academic," meaning what pertains to a university, joined to (2) "discipline," meaning how we know what we want to know about any subject.

So I here set up two things that, in former times, cannot have been juxtaposed. I confuse two formerly separate classifications, "Jewish learning," and "academic disciplines." "Jewish learning," formerly of self-evident value to both insider and outsider (though the assessments differed), now has to win a hearing for itself, but now has the chance to do so. "Academic disciplines," formerly extended to only what was familiar, or near at hand—the history of England and America, the Spanish and French languages, the philosophy of the West, the social-scientific study of people like us—now move outward. Universities in particular reach toward what is unfamiliar, yet precious to some among us, the history of Armenia or Latin America or Poland; the Hebrew or Chinese or Arabic languages; the social-scientific study of people unlike us in the color of their skin, not to mention their literature and humanity.

So too, academic disciplines now exercise judgment upon books that formerly stood in elegant majesty, all by themselves. Historians of late antiquity want to know what they may learn from the Talmuds. More important, young people in search of an education will take up Judaism, though they are not Jews or are Jews with no prior intellectual commitments to Jewish learning. Just as all of the new subjects find their place in the curriculum, alongside wholly new methods and procedures, so even new disciplines are aborning. Some subjects are fading away. Other new topics, or old ones learned in new ways, come to the fore.

Now that the problem confronting the authors of these papers is clear, I need not preview their results or restate them. The authors

Introduction

speak for themselves. Each one was asked to explain something of what is happening in his subject within the disciplinary setting of a university. The question to each was this: What do you teach? How do you teach it when you take up the education of future professors? Smith begins the work, showing that what I do in studying Judaism, he does in studying Christianity. Alter and Band make clear that issues confronting comparative literature in the fields of French and Russian literature also engage the imagination of scholars who work on Hebrew literature. Important even in the discussion of method is the matter of substantive results—as Goldscheider and Zuckerman demonstrate. Some contributors choose not merely to *tell*, but also to *show*, what happens when an old subject moves to a new setting. Levine is one instance here. To others, like Fox, what the student has to know to do the job requires and receives the most detailed attention. Still others regard the matter of how the graduate educator relates to the students as the critical focus. Raphael takes that view, which seems to me a valid definition of how to describe change. For the relationship of master to disciple is not the same as the relationship of apprentice to craftsman or of mature researcher to young but highly qualified beginner. And relationships among learning people serve, in their way, as accurate indicators of change. The topic is a painful one, but cannot be treated as irrelevant to the larger phenomenon at hand.

I do not claim we have done more than open discussion and explore in a preliminary way the things we might discuss, the ways in which we might carry on discourse. We speak of a phenomenon of scarcely two decades. Even if we make reference to American and Canadian precursors to the present development of Jewish learning in our universities, hence to the disciplinary modes of organization definitive of research and teaching here, we encompass not a hundred years of a tradition of learning that goes back, in Judaism, for nearly two thousand, and, in the academy, for nearly one thousand. So the union is between aged and irreconcilable parents. And we do not yet know what, if any, offspring can result.

Yet even now, it is clear, the pedigree will prove a problem. Those of us who today dominate university studies in Jewish learning mostly come from Jewish parents. In many cases we even studied in *yeshivot* or in rabbinical schools before going to graduate school. Some earned

Introduction

doctorates in rabbinical seminaries to begin with. In former times, people who knew the things we know and taught the things we now teach were transformed in the social imagination of the Jewish people into holy men. All the students were Jews and aspired, also, to become holy men. But today our students are as commonly non-Jews as Jews, and, if Jews, as commonly marginal to their Jewish origins as engaged by them. We teach in universities, and so, by definition, we teach anyone who comes into our classrooms, without regard to race, creed, color. We are responsible for only a small part of their education.

So although we spend our lives studying Jewish holy books and there is no more particularly Jewish activity than what we do, yet it is accurate to describe us as standing outside of the community of Judaism. Among the available categories, rabbi or "professional" or lay leader, there is no place for us. True, there *is* room for learned Jews. But they are received as eccentrics or turned into Hebrew teachers. There is no room in Jewry for a learned Jew who makes a living by teaching what he or she knows, on the one side, but who is paid for doing so by secular, neutral institutions, on the other.

We Jewish professors of Jewish learning are like our field. We fall within no frame of available norms. People do not know what to make of us. We are authorities without responsibility, leaders without a constituency. We speak but no one said we might. And none can silence us. We are listened to. Rabbis in general are supposed to be learned, but they are pretty much under the thumb of lay leaders and know it. Accordingly, they are Jewish authorities but responsible to their boards and members. They lead a specific constituency. Other sorts of Jewish professionals are paid not for what they know but for what they can do; they surely are not much like us.

The ironies are not merely social and political. These merely symbolize the real anomaly. People (men) who study the holy books in *yeshivot* become holy by studying them, different from other people. But except in so far as professors of physics, economics, or religious studies alike are different from "nonprofessors," there is no difference between us professors of Jewish studies and anyone else. At least, there is no difference founded in particular upon the things we know and others do not know. I suppose we might say that those who teach in *yeshivot* go to heaven because of what they know and do. Judaism's conception of heaven, after all, is a *yeshiva* on high. We too enjoy whatever heaven there is and is apt to be. But it is here and now. That is to say, knowing and doing the things that are ours, in the place in which we find ourselves—the university—is all we want and all we ever wanted, thus: heaven.

Moreover, it would be banal to say that what we do in a university is to "study Torah." Insofar as that is true, it simply means that under secular, neutral auspices we read the same books, learn the same texts, that rabbis learn under Jewish auspices. It would be a cliché to say that, wherever they are studied, the books are holy because of their contents. That is so. But it hardly matters. For the attitudes brought to books, the questions one wishes to answer, surely define the things one will learn from them. It would be an evasion to allege that we merely turn up interesting things about the ancient Jews, as though we read the texts as testimonies to what dead people said in a long-distant past. This world knows antiquarians, but few of them in universities. Intellectually and morally, universities are far too vigorous and engaged places to sustain knowledge "for its own sake." That is to say, we aim at far more than the triviality of knowing merely one thing after another. To us the texts live. They address vital issues of our day, issues about which we all care. They are important, not merely interesting. If what makes a book holy is that its message is received as truth, a kind of revelation, then to us the texts we study are holy. But that is the only sense. And it is not a sense that falls in the category of Torah. We professors of Jewish studies do not see ourselves as apostles, or even as exemplars, of Judaism. Nor, happily, are we perceived that way. Whole platoons of aggrieved students can hate us without being anti-Semites. Students learn from us without finding the path to the *miqveh* for conversion to Judaism, if they are non-Jews, or without buying two sets of dishes and giving up lobster, if they are Jews.

Ours is a secular task. It is secular because it is personal, not collective. We speak in our own names, not in the name of Judaism—let alone Torah, or God. It is not possible to take a more secular stance, in the context of Judaism, than to sign one's own name to one's books. The very individuality represented by the creative scholar—the one who thinks thoughts not thought before and does not submit them for the approbation of the keepers of the grail—

violates the collective and traditional Judaic traditions on learning. The secularity, however, derives from more than the mere affirmation of individuality.

So far as we are concerned, the holy books of Judaism (or any other books) are important not in themselves, but because of what they tell us about what is important: they answer urgent questions of humanity. The *givenness* of the importance of one text, rather than some other (to Jews, a Torah text; to Marxists, a letter of Engels; to Christians, a Gospel; to professors of English, a given poem or play or novel), is never to be conceded. A text bears no intrinsic value, no self-evidence. To win attention, a text must not merely demand it (or, more accurately, have a holy, or otherwise authoritative, personality demand it). A text is judged by its power of exemplification. That is why, exercising taste and judgment, all of us are the arbiters of life and death to otherwise dead books and ideas. Note that the issue is not merely to contrast the gullibility of the pietists with the critical and detached judgment of scholars. Nor shall the ignorant and easy distinction between the smart secular and the dumb religious be permitted. Anyone who has studied the texts on which we labor is not apt to agree that the framers and students of the texts we study are anything but brilliant and intellectually vital and able. The point of differentiation lies elsewhere entirely.

If the value of a text is not self-evident, so that one may claim everyone should know it as part of a general literacy, it is because, in the neutral and secular setting of universities, claims of special revelation are set aside. But these, then, do not give way to equivalently private and parochial claims based on taste and judgment: "This is what I like." What is operative is the criterion of general intelligibility. That is to say, what speaks merely to this one's whim and that one's capacity for being charmed lays no claim on everyone's intellect. What does demand careful reading, reflection, and response is what attempts to speak to one and all. In the nature of things, that is the text with the power to exemplify a large and accessible human perplexity. In universities, open to all as they should be, what we principally aim at is intelligible discourse, conversation with others. The bridge is reason, shared modes of thought. The goal is learning what is in the mind (not to exclude the heart and sentiment) of the other party, the other group. True, in working at the task of shared intelligibility, the power of common discourse, we too form a distinct group in society, the (employed) intellectuals. But that is not the purpose of our rites. Our rituals are not meant solely to validate our group. We wish to dissolve the boundaries of privacy and parochial self-evidence in favor of enlarging the range of mutual comprehension and deeper understanding. Our labor, therefore, is to create what is most particular to, and private in, a given social culture, I mean, a language. But the language must be one accessible to the generality of humanity—whatever languages they speak. If we cannot speak the accessible language of reason, we end up talking to ourselves. How to shape a suitable language, how to ask questions, the answers to which someone outside of a narrow circle of adepts or specialists or a captive audience of believers might want— that is the challenge of our universities.

The distinction, therefore, between our learning, in universities, and other people's learning, elsewhere than in universities, is as follows.

First, we learn not merely to discover facts—though we do make discoveries—but to make sense of facts.

Second, we learn not merely because the thing we learn self-evidently is there to be learned. We learn because we can say there is something important in the thing we learn: because it answers urgent questions.

Third, the criterion of success or failure of discourse among us is general intelligibility, the power to address a large and varied world out of the resources of that small thing we know better than anyone else. As Jonathan Z. Smith says of the proper study of religions:

> For the self-conscious student of religion, no datum possesses intrinsic interest. It is of value only in so far as it can serve as *exempli gratia* of some fundamental issue in the imagination of religion. The student of religion must be able to articulate clearly why "this" rather than "that" was chosen as an exemplum. His primary skill is concentrated in this choice. This effort at articulate choice is all the more difficult, and hence all the more necessary, for the historian of religions who accepts the boundaries neither of canon nor of community in constituting his intellectual domain, in providing his range of exempla.

Introduction

Implicit in this effort at articulate choice are three conditions. First, that the exemplum has been well and fully understood. This requires a mastery of both the relevant primary material and the history and tradition of its interpretation. Second, that the exemplum be displayed in the service of some important theory, some paradigm, some fundamental question, some central element in the academic imagination of religion. Third, that there be some method for explicitly relating the exemplum to the theory, paradigm, or question and some method for evaluating each in terms of the other.

What Smith says about the study of religions constitutes the contemporary program and platform for the humanities and social sciences in general. We believe that what people know and think, how they use their minds, define the fundamental condition of being human. We believe that the capacity to know and think is common, leading to shared perceptions, susceptible of interpretation and criticism. We think people can and should talk with one another through reason about reasoned propositions, and that, through thought, they can distinguish good from bad. Knowing leads to criticism, judgment, the exercise of reasoned taste. The theological affirmation of the human condition says it all in a single sentence: "When you eat of it, your eyes will be opened, and you will be like God, knowing good and evil." We have tasted. Insofar as we claim to know the difference between good and bad, we act like God, and appropriately so, created as we are in God's image. When we give up that claim and treat one opinion as no better or worse than any other, when we make things up as we go along and call it truth or learning, we are no longer like God.

So, in the end, the Jewish scholar of Jewish studies in the heavenly university I have described embodies the situation of Israel among the nations: like and not like, common and unique, never sure whether Balaam's blessing was not, in the end, a curse: "a people dwelling alone, and not reckoning itself among the nations." If Israel is sui generis, then it has no place on this earth. If it is like the nations, then how can it be different, dwelling alone? What does it mean to be different? If what we teach is holy, then it surely cannot be common. Why should someone not a Jew want to know it? But if a Jew, why should someone not engaged by Judaism, and then a very special and particular brand of Judaism at that, want to study it? If we are not apostles or exemplars, what relationship do we have to the subject we teach? In phrasing matters in this academic way, I have simply refocused and so reframed the issues of Jewish existence perceived, from afar to be sure, by the one who came to curse and stayed to bless.

Squarely upon the boundaries between one thing and something else—this defines the circumstances of Israel, the Jewish people. But it is not Israel alone that lives on the margins, but also humanity and society, hence the humanities and social sciences alike. How so? Every individual is different from every other individual. Each group defines in its own terms and classifications those traits that make it a group—who stands inside, who is outside. The particular point of insistence of a given society or culture—the Jews on food, the Catholics on sex, to speak in vulgar terms—bears nothing in common with the particular point of insistence of some other. Theologians claim not only that their religion constitutes the true religion, but also that their terms and classifications constitute the embodiment of religion; everything else is something else. Or, to the contrary, theirs is not a religion; everything else is.

In this context it is not banal to observe that, while everyone is special, we normally have two eyes, two arms, two legs, one brain, one heart. It is then a norm of the human condition to speculate on how we are special and how we are the same—and never to know the ultimate result of the speculation. That is the nature of human society. It is the condition of the individual. It is what all of us have in common.

It is hardly surprising, therefore, that a group so chronically marginal and acutely self-conscious as the Jews, in their own view barometers of culture and society because of their very sense of marginality, should wonder about these things. It follows that the human condition is exemplified by the curious situation of the Jewish scholar of Jewish studies: coming from the group and yet speaking to a larger world, intimate with the most particular and special learning of the Jewish people, yet bringing to that body of learning the questions of general intelligibility.

Now to the essays at hand. How are we to bring young people,

Introduction

Jews and others as well, to that marginal condition, that moment rich in possibilities, in which learning in Judaic studies turns them into paradigms for humanity, the professors of Judaic studies of the coming age? Let me close this effort to place into proper perspective the move from *yeshiva* to university. How shall we assess the value of the move? In my view the sole interesting criterion is whether or not, in this new and unfamiliar world, we do at least as well as our forefathers did in the old and experienced one. For *yeshivot* have passed the test of nearly eighteen hundred years of educational effort: they did, and do, take seriously and at face value the work of learning. They did, and do, celebrate what a person knows and how he knows it. They care, therefore, about the thing that counts. When our students, educated in a different way for a different world to be sure, are famed for their sheer erudition and personal commitment to the ongoing processes of learning, as were, and are *yeshiva* students, then, but only then, shall we have claim and cause to celebrate. True, we take seriously the tasks of the new age, as well as the wisdom and intellectual achievements of the old, enduring one. But, old world and new alike, only one thing in the end matters to education: the learning itself. So I do not know whether the shift in the social world of the Jewish intellect at its most particular and Judaic, from one society and institution to another, is a good thing. I only know how, in time to come, we shall be able to tell.

Part One

The Academic Study of Judaism

1. Modes of Jewish Studies in the University

Jacob Neusner

Learning constitutes a central religious category in Judaism. From the earliest days of rabbinic Judaism almost to the present time, "study of Torah" predominated, in various forms, in shaping the values of the Jews. The present-day academies in which "Torah" is studied claim descent from schools first founded in Palestine well before the third century B.C. and in Babylonia in the second century A.D. The books written in those schools and the conventions and canons of inquiry originally laid down there continue to occupy students in traditional schools. Among the intellectual traditions which took shape in the Middle East in late antiquity, the Jewish one thrives much in the old way, as well as in new forms, and represents one of the longest unbroken chains of learning among humanity, along with Confucianism and the study of philosophy.

The advent of the study of Judaism in American universities must be seen from this perspective. Judaism is no parvenu in the world of the academy. The scholar whose main task is the study of Judaism may be a relative newcomer in the American university, for until the late 1950s only a few faculties provided for appointments in the subject of postbiblical Jewish learning. But there is nothing at all novel about scholarly study of, or within, Judaism. If scholars have received sufficient training in the classical tradition, its sources and methods, then they have become new representatives of a very old tradition of learning. I stress this point, not because antiquity by itself confers any great prestige, but rather because today some Jews celebrate their "acceptance" by the universities of America, as if they had done little or nothing to deserve it. Given both their reverence for learning and veritable awe of the learned man, and also the persistence of these religious traits in cultural and secular forms, they bring to the university a rich appreciation of its central tasks, and their tradition makes its contribution as well. But the university as we know it is only the most recent, and at present not by any means the most important, setting for the enterprise of the Jewish intellect.

My purpose here is not to argue the thesis that Jewish studies belong within the university curriculum, but rather, first, to analyze briefly what these studies comprehend, second, to distinguish between modes of Jewish learning in universities and in Jewish schools, and finally to adumbrate the place I believe appropriate for Jewish studies within the study of religions. (A second, equally important place, in Near Eastern studies, is not under discussion here.)

Definition: What Is Included in University Studies

We must first carefully define the various modes of Jewish learning so that we may be able to distinguish those germane to universities from those most useful in parochial, Jewish schools. It is clear that the wide range of Jewish studies exhibits a mixture of presuppositions, methods, and topics of interest. Not all of these would contribute to university studies of religion. Furthermore, it is obvious that, when Jews study themselves and their own traditions, they naturally rely upon unarticulated assumptions and exhibit implicit attitudes which require specification. After examining the several definitions for Jewish learning, we shall then be in a position to separate the aspects of Judaic studies appropriate for universities from those best cultivated in Jewish seminaries.

What do we mean by Jewish studies? To answer this question, one must define "study of Torah," *Wissenschaft des Judenthums,* "Hebraica," "Hebrew studies," "Judaica," "Jewish learning," and other terms used to denote the subject under discussion. Of these terms, the broadest is "Jewish learning," which includes the systematic study of the beliefs, actions, and literary and cultural products of all persons who have been called, or have called themselves, "Jews" (of which more below). Within "Jewish learning" one may discern sev-

Modes of Jewish Studies

eral fairly distinct categories. First is "study of Torah," the traditional, religiously motivated activity, developed over the centuries and focused upon study of the Talmud, commentaries, legal codes, rabbinic interpretation of the Hebrew Bible, and similar sacred sciences pursued in classical Jewish academies and seminaries. Second is "Hebraica" or "Hebrew studies," the study of the Hebrew language, biblical, cognate, and, more recently, modern literature, and related subjects, which was undertaken in American universities and Protestant divinity schools from the very beginning, and now continues in departments of Near Eastern languages and literatures, linguistics, or comparative literature. Third is "Judaica," the systematic study of Judaism, its history and theology, law and practices, and of the Jews as a group, generally carried on in departments of religion or in the social sciences. Of these modes of Jewish learning, the third is the one that will be discussed here. The divisions within "Jewish studies" are rarely demarcated by such clear-cut boundaries as those I have suggested. In general, university programs in "Jewish learning" are divided between Near Eastern and religious studies.[1]

Adequate definitions for the terms "Jew," "Jewish," "Judaism" and "Judaic" are required as well. The study of Judaism includes its philosophy and theology, religious literature, art, music, law, dance, and history; a "Judaic" study focuses upon some aspect of Judaism as a religion. The study of the Jews concerns the culture, sociology, politics, languages, art, literature, and other artifacts of the distinct historical group of that name. That group is composed of people who were born of a Jewish mother, or converted to Judaism. I offer the definition of the Jew given by Jewish law. One may broaden it slightly by adding that a Jew is one who thinks he is, or is thought by others to be, Jewish, with the qualification that such belief is not based upon mistaken facts. Whether or not one may isolate qualities which are distinctively "Jewish" is not at issue here.[2]

In this definition one must stress the importance of change. Qualities or features which Jews borrowed from other peoples in one setting frequently became rooted in Judaism or Jewry, so that later on, or elsewhere, they came to be seen as peculiarly Judaic or Jewish. The Jewish calendar, that "unique" construction of Judaism, derives mostly from the Canaanites. It may be argued that the festivals were "monotheized" or "Judaized," but in fact different verbal explanations have been imposed on the same festivals celebrating the same natural phenomena of the same Palestinian agricultural year. In the early days of Reform Judaism, it was thought that, if one uncovered the "origin" of a practice or belief, we might then decide whether it was "essential" or peripheral. Nowadays there is less interest in "origins." The exposure of the genetic fallacy may have been part of the reason for this shift: it was quickly recognized that determination of the origin does not exhaust the meaning of a belief or practice. Yet there was another source as well. For it has been progressively more difficult, with the advance of scholarship, to discover *any* deeply "Jewish" or "Israelite" practice which was not in some degree the creation of some other culture or civilization. The Jews, over long centuries, have assumed as their own what was produced originally by others, and their infinite adaptability has been made possible by short memories and tenacious insistence on the mythic-Jewish origins of purely gentile or pagan customs. Whatever was or was not Jewish, a great many things have *become* so.

So far I have not alluded to peculiar Jewish disciplines or methods of study, although these exist, some people suppose, in Talmudic dialectic. That dialectic, however, is formed of Roman principles of legal codification and Greek principles of rhetoric. Probably one could find numerous parallels among contemporary Syriac, Late Babylonian, and Hellenistic traditions, if these were sufficiently well known to us, just as the Jewish academies have their parallels. Although a discipline may be peculiar to a tradition of learning and still be derivative, I doubt that over a long period of time Jewish learning can be associated with any particular discipline, in the sense that sociology has its methods, or physics its procedures. Obviously Jewish learning can lay no persuasive claim to exclusive possession of subtlety or cleverness, devotion to the intellectual life, dedication to "matters of the spirit," or any of the other traits—pejorative or complimentary—claimed for it by its religious and secular enemies or apologists.

"Jewish learning," broadly construed, is most nearly analogous, in university terms, to an *area* study, in which various disciplines, drawn from the humanities, such as philology, art history, musicology, or literary criticism, and from the social sciences, such as political science, economics, sociology, or the like, are brought to bear upon a certain region, or nation, or segment of society. "Jewish learning" does not necessarily fit into a special department, though "Judaica" appropriately belongs in a department of religious studies, "Hebrew studies" or Hebraica in a department of Near Eastern languages, and "Jewish studies" pursued from a historical or sociological perspective in a department of history or sociology or anthropology. Just as many methods may be profitably applied to the study of a geographical region, so also many methods may be used to elucidate aspects of the study of the Jews as a group or of Judaism as a religion. Specialists in various areas of Jewish learning may be located in different departments. In addition, *centers* of interdisciplinary programs of Jewish learning, in which specialists from several disciplines may be brought together to work on the Jewish and Judaic materials, ought to be created, where feasible. Such "institutes of Jewish studies" would be analogous to the Russian Institute at Columbia and the Middle East Institute at Harvard. On the other hand, a *department* of Jewish or Judaic studies seems to me a misnomer, for departments normally take shape around particular disciplines or approaches to data. Even though departmental and disciplinary lines are breaking down, it is still important to structure Jewish studies in universities according to appropriate existing principles of academic organization.

So far as it is necessary in the beginning to select certain modes of Jewish learning for university purposes, I think two are primary: concentration in Hebrew language and literature for Near Eastern or comparative literature departments, and in the history of Judaism for departments of religious studies. I see no role whatever for the Judaica specialist in the study of contemporary philosophy, though of course studies in the history of philosophy will require his or her contribution. The social scientist normally makes use of all kinds of data, deriving them from many different cultures, traditions, and social groups, without specializing in any of them. I should suppose, therefore, that the various social sciences, especially anthropology, sociology, and psychology, would find the inclusion of a "specialist in the Jews" egregious and wasteful.

Whether history belongs to the social sciences or the humanities, I see a limited place for the Jewish historian *as such* in as history department. In the past, to be sure, general histories of the Jews have been written, and one might thereby be led to suppose that "the Jews," as a single entity (or "people") existing in various times and places, have had a single history, in the same way as England or America or China has had a history. It seems to me that the normal inquiry of historians proceeds on the assumption—whether upon geographical, or political, or sociological grounds—that what one is dealing with is a single entity which has had a history. To suppose that "the Jews" constitute such an entity or "people" requires, first of all, assent to a theological or ideological judgment. Once that step is taken, however, the morphology of one's further studies has been established. Whether or not it is congruent with that of historical studies is an open question.

A specialist in Jewish history presumably must be trained not merely in historical *method*, but also in the data pertaining to his field, data which in the Jewish case extend over more countries, cultures, and centuries than most scholars are capable of mastering. The specialist in Jewish history who works in late antiquity has to reckon with Jews who spoke several languages and lived in several different political systems, who wrote many kind of books, preserved afterward among many different and conflicting groups, each of which claimed to be "the Jews" or "Israel" from that time forward. When Jewish historians proceed to medieval studies, they must once again face the variety and breadth of Jewish data, and so too in the modern period. Whether or not a single historian can specialize in "the Balkans" or "the Middle East" and achieve the mastery of the many languages, literatures, and histories demanded, I think it unlikely that the same could be done in a thoroughly professional manner with the Jews. Both unarticulated ideological or theological and technical or methodological problems stand in the way of Jewish history.

If, on the other hand, scholars working, for example, mainly in medieval European history specialize in Jewish materials, as others may stress Gemany, or Italy, or Poland, they may make a very significant contribution. For they become acquainted at the same time with the broader cultural and social environment which shaped the lives of all people, including the Jews, in medieval Europe; they deepen understanding of the various political and economic systems governing all groups in a given territory, including the Jews, and learn about the literature, religion, and other aspects of the civiliza-

Modes of Jewish Studies 9

tion of those among whom Jews lived over a period of several centuries. They deal with a specialty within a broader field of historical research, just as others do. They are not expected to do more than can reasonably be asked of them. They can become expert, and, reaching the frontiers of knowledge at a few specific points, may cross over into unexplored territory.

I do not see how the thirty or forty centuries generally included under the rubric of "Jewish history" can be adequately studied by any one person, and I do not think professional scholarship can cope with so broad a temporal range of study, even within a relatively narrow frame of reference. The need to know the whole of a single period will prevent the historian from knowing the rest of the history of the Jews. In larger faculties, where several scholars may concentrate upon a single period, such as medieval or modern Europe, there should be a specialist in Jewish material, just as there is in French, Italian, or Russian. But, in general, Jewish history seems to me a less manageable field than the history of Judaism (of which more below).

The contrary expectation supposes that the study of Jewish history may safely exclude careful attention to the affairs of the societies among which Jews were living. The presupposition is that these affairs had little or nothing to do with Jewish religion, culture, sociology, literature, and the like. From the Canaanites to the Americans, massive testimony to the contrary has accrued, with variation, but without exception. It is, moreover, a theological judgment to include in Jewish history the study of "normative Jews" and their culture and to exclude the history of others, such as various sorts of Christians, Karaites, and Sabbateans, who from their origins on have claimed to be "the Jews" or "Israel." Whether or not such a judgment can be made, it certainly ought to be made—and put into effect—by *historians*. So there is, or should be, no such field of specialization as Jewish history and, hence, no place in a department of history for a specialist in Jewish history. Places obviously should be found for a medievalist, or a modernist in European or even American studies, and certainly a specialist in ancient history, who works mainly, though not exclusively, on Jewish sources. All those who do specialize in the nonspecialty known as Jewish history in fact end up, as is entirely proper and necessary, concentrating on a particular time period and geographical region, and frequently on only one aspect of Jewish history of that circumscribed time and place.³

Modes of Jewish Studies outside the University: Study of Torah

What is the relationship between university-based Jewish studies discussed above and studies in a Jewish school? The place of Jewish learning in universities is necessarily conditioned by the universe of discourse existing within the university. As I said in the Introduction, the university attempts to bring into relationship with one another many kinds of area studies and many sorts of disciplines, in both the humanities and the social sciences. In the context of this heteronomous discourse within the university, various bodies of knowledge contribute to the elucidation of questions of common interest. Under these circumstances Jewish studies are required to concentrate on those elements that are of interest to other disciplines or areas. But the classical tradition of Jewish learning contains many elements that are of no interest at all to outsiders. Pursued for their own sake, that is to say, as an autonomous body of tradition and knowledge dependent upon no other scholarly tradition and no other body of questions or perspectives for validation or relevance, Jewish studies have quite another type of existence. Seeing matters from this standpoint, we may come to a clearer understanding of the relationship between a given area of study and those who actually *live* in the area which is under study.

Within the community of the faithful, Jewish studies from late antiquity onward have focused upon the study of the traditions regarded as having been revealed at Mt. Sinai to Moses (according to Talmudic belief) in both oral and written form. The written revelation is contained in the Pentateuch and, beyond that, in the prophetic books and the writings supposed also to have been written under divine inspiration. The oral tradition was finally written down in the form of the Palestinian and Babylonian Talmuds, various collections of scriptural exegeses known as *midrashim,* and cognate literature. Other literature produced by Jews in the long period from Ezra to Mohammed, circa 440 B.C. to A.D. 640, was not preserved by the rabbinical schools and was not therefore included within the scope of the term "Torah." From the Islamic conquest of the Middle East and the subsequent fructification of all fields of human thought, "Torah" expanded, even in rabbinical circles, to embrace the disciplines of philosophy and metaphysics. From the tenth century to the fifteenth, a vigorous philosophical tradition took shape under the impact of Moslem rationalism. Still a third mode of premodern Jewish studies existed in the form of Kabbalah, the Jewish mystical tradition, which conceived of "Torah" under a wholly new guise, as an arcane doctrine of metaphysical mythology. A fourth form was the legal and ethical tradition. This was pursued, first, through commentary upon the Babylonian Talmud, second, through legal research resulting in the issuance of a *responsum* (a letter in reply to a specific legal question), or in the provision of a court decision, and, third, through the construction of great codes of Jewish law, bringing up to date and organizing by specific principles the discrete corpora of laws then being developed in particular countries and by various authorities. A fifth form, which was liturgical and in a measure belletristic, resulted in the composition of a great body of poetry, both religious and secular, in the Hebrew language. A sixth was Bible study and commentary. Of the modes of Jewish learning in premodern times, biblical-Talmudic studies were by far the most common; the others existed in small and relatively isolated, uninfluential circles, except at specific times and for local reasons.

The birth of *Wissenschaft des Judenthums* among the nineteenth-century German Jews who had received both a classical Jewish and a university education added to the range of Jewish studies several modern sciences. These were, specifically, history, philology, textual criticism of the classical texts, and biblical studies in the modern mode.[4] New, also, and of greater importance, were the attitudes of complete freedom of interpretation as well as, in Glatzer's words, of "freedom from the possible application of the results of scholarship to the conduct of life." A further change, Glatzer points out, was from the exegetical to the abstract mode of discourse. No longer were books called "contributions toward" or "comments on," but instead major comprehensive projects were undertaken. Most recently, sociology and contemporary history have begun to take root in a particularly Jewish academic environment. Furthermore, books formerly ignored by Jews but preserved by Christians, such as the biblical apocrypha and the New Testament, Josephus, Philo, and the like, have reentered the framework of Jewish learning in modern times.

What unites classical and modern sciences of Judaism are the convictions, first, that such an entity as a "Jewish people" exists, which permits one to study as a *unity* the literature, history, and other cultural artifacts of people who lived in widely separated places and epochs; second, that sufficient unity pervades the culture so that one may meaningfully write a history of Jewish (as opposed merely to modern Hebrew) literature, or a history of the Jews, or similar compositions; and, third, that scholarship concerning "the Jewish people," its culture and religion and history, even its languages, is intrinsically important and interesting. Most significant of all, Jewish studies carried on in an autonomous framework presuppose not only their own intrinsic interest and importance but also their worth in molding the values of the living generation, whether these be religious or secular (*Wissenschaft des Judenthums* was not a university discipline—though it aspired to academic status—but the creation of the early Reformers of Judaism who, despite disclaimers, intended through it to point the way toward the future development of the faith.) Jewish studies in Jewish institutions, therefore, are pursued not simply because they may illuminate some aspect of the humanities or social sciences but, especially and immediately, because they will help the Jewish student to form his beliefs and values by reference to the tradition of which he is a part, or, more descriptively, which shaped his forefathers in various ways.

In my view, any cultural or religious tradition has the right to be taken seriously in its *own* terms, and especially by those to whom it addresses itself. It is not enough to study the traditions and lore of the Jews as aspects of humanity, or because they may provide significant insight into the human condition. The rhetoric may be appealing, but the results are disastrous to scholarship. All specificities, all boundaries, all possibility of commitment are quite properly destroyed when the particularities of Jewish learning are subsumed under, and then blotted out by, the perspectives of the humanities or social sciences. It is one thing to study Yiddish, Judaeo-Arabic, Judaeo-Persian, or Hebrew at various points in history because they

Modes of Jewish Studies

represent interesting data for the linguist, a valid and important perspective. But it is quite another to study the various languages Jews have regarded as Jewish in order to come to a deeper understanding of their values or of the way their languages generate and interpret visions of reality, or even in order to learn to express oneself through them. The linguist may learn to make use of one of the many languages he studies; the philologist may penetrate into the deeper meaning of a word; but only the committed student and his equally devoted teacher want to *use* that language and find a deeper means of self-expression through that use. Yiddish or Hebrew may well be studied by linguists or Orientalists, respectively, but the value of studying them is quite different, more personal and, I think, more profound, when believing Jews in an autonomous and self-contained setting learn them. Jewish studies represent a heteronomous body of learning; but they also constitute an antonomous tradition, with its own claims and value statements. To ignore the latter is to render impossible the success of the former.

I argue, therefore, that certain kinds of Jewish studies belong within the university curriculum, others only within Jewish institutions of higher learning (such as seminaries and institutes for advanced study), and some in both. Rather than specify particular branches of Jewish studies appropriate for each setting, I offer the particular criteria in terms of which judgments should be made. To generalize, potentially each branch of Jewish learning has a contribution to make to university studies, and the criterion for incorporation into the university curriculum will be the possibility of applying university methods of study to the particular subject matters(s). To take one example: the Talmud deserves to be studied in the classical, dialectical manner. It was composed with just such study in mind, and when deprived of the richness of commentary, scholastic disquisition, and the search for new insights in the perfectly traditional, old-fashioned modes, it loses its integrity. That is to say, study of the Talmud must be "study of Torah." But at the same time the Talmud is a historical document. Thus it may be viewed as a resource for philological and cultural studies, as evidence for the state of religion, economic life, sociology, and politics in ancient times, and as a repository of values which in various ways have continued to guide the life of the Jews. For social-scientific purposes, the Talmud (as much as the Church Fathers) provides data of great interest for inquiry in the tradition of Max Weber and Ernst Troeltsch, to name only two sociologists of religion. I see no connection between classical Talmud study and the university curriculum, but many relationships between Talmudic literature and various university studies in both the humanities and social sciences.

I think it unfortunate that the success of Jewish studies within the university rests, as it has for a century, upon that of Jewish studies outside it. The mastery of the necessary languages and classical disciplines required for advanced scholarship in Jewish materials cannot be acquired in a few years or in a few courses. Jewish learning demands too deep an education for advanced work to be undertaken upon a foundation presently existing in university curricula alone. Today, therefore, Jewish studies, both in the history of Judaism and in the languages, literature, and history and sociology of the Jews, depend upon extrauniversity resources. At the present time it may well be advantageous for the scholar of many Jewish subjects to be a Jew in origin and upbringing. The insufficiency of university facilities, and not the intrinsic character of the subject, is the cause. I think that the university must fully carry out its responsibilities, so that a person entering with no background in, or even contact with, the subject may within the normal period of years emerge as a suitably qualified scholar. Thus the university will preserve its own autonomy and achieve that self-sufficiency which in the end will protect and maintain its character. No subject taught in a university must ultimately depend upon foundations laid outside of it. Of course, university-based scholars of Judaica must make maximum use of the substantial achievements of modern scholarship, which has produced the translations, concordances, critical texts, and scientific commentaries needed to provide somewhat easier access to documents, mastery of which would otherwise require a lifetime of study.

On the other hand, one can hardly consign extrauniversity Jewish learning to the sterility or boredom of the old issues, forms, and procedures. The same problems which led to the development of contemporary humanities and social-scientific scholarship within the university are just as troublesome outside of it. Indeed, the philological, historical, social-scientific, and other methods hammered out in the past century provide as useful a tool for analysis of a text in a seminary classroom as in a university. One may, of course, continue to ask the old questions and carry out the old procedures. Proof of this possibility derives from the actuality of Jewish learning in more than a few Jewish institutions of higher learning. But the old questions seem less troubling, and the old answers of diminishing persuasiveness. If we find a key to treasures of insight, it should open many doors. The newer modes of learning need, therefore, to reshape the older ones.

Let me make the difference between modes of learning in a university and in other centers of study more explicit. Scholars in universities do not differ from their counterparts in Jewish-sponsored schools of higher learning in commitment, concern, or protagonism. But the focus of commitment and concern is radically different. The university scholar seeks understanding of structures, the parochial scholar (and I do not use the word pejoratively) seeks participation in them. In a university, commitment is to the scholarly method or result; in a parochial institution, to the content of what is studied. In a university, concern is for humanity or society first, to a particular segment or example of it second; in the parochial institution, concern is for the group first, mankind afterward. Protagonism in the parochial institution is taken for granted. In the university, one advocates scholarly alternatives; but the act of advocacy of a religion as such will impede the comprehension of a religion other than one's own, and I suspect it will also impede understanding of one's own religion. In the parochial center of learning, the significance of the opinion or perspective on the external environment, although one can hardly claim to ignore or exclude it, cannot be so decisive as the opinion and perspective on the tradition itself.

From the university perspective on "reality," it is impossible to locate "the Jewish people"; what comes into view are only various groups called "Jewish," a term bearing various meanings in diverse settings and serving particular functions within different societies. Thus, to one outside the tradition, "the Jews" as a group are best defined functionally and episodically. In the Jewish school, on the other hand, "the Jewish people" loses its quotation marks. From their own viewpoint believing Jews cannot deny the reality of Jewish history. Indeed, in Jewish schools "the Jewish people" constitutes a central category of analysis, on a par with Jewish Law, the God of

Abraham, Isaac, and Jacob, or the hope for the end of days and the advent of the Messiah. Thus "Jewish history" represents a vital field of study in Jewish seminaries, for in that context peoplehood as a construct serves to unify the otherwise discrete and disparate data concerning the Jews. "Jewish history" provides a chief source for the verification and validation of theological or ideological convictions in an institution so defined. The appeal to the past, together with the recognition of the authority of some in it, is the presupposition of religious thought for those who are Jewish by identity.

Judaism within the History of Religions

What is the role of Jewish studies in the history of religions? The techniques of the history of religions and its categories of analysis have been applied unflinchingly, mostly by scholars of Christian descent, to every religious tradition of mankind, both archaic and modern, except for two, Christianity and Judaism. Of the two, Judaism is still less studied than Christianity. To be sure, the scriptures of ancient Israel have undergone religious-historical study, and the Jewish sectarian environment between the Maccabees and the first century A.D. (including the early Church) has been carefully examined from many perspectives. Yet practically no work has been done, except by a very few individuals, on the history of Judaism since that time. No subdivision within the history of religions known as "history of Judaism" has yet come into existence. The reason is that, for Christianity, "history of religions" was really meant to provide a means of studying the religions of the Orient. The history of Judaism was clearly to be subsumed within the "Judaeo-Christian tradition," which for theological reasons was not to be subjected to the same kind of analyses. The "Judaeo" part of the Judaeo-Christian tradition, according to this conception, usually drops away about A.D. 70, but never later than A.D. 135. Similarly, in Protestant and nonsectarian schools, the "Roman Catholic" part of the "Western" Christian tradition (or, under secular auspices, "civilization") ends at the Reformation. Such extraordinary events in the history of Roman Catholicism as the nineteenth-century renaissance somehow find little, if any, place in histories of Western "Judaeo-Christianity."

Modes of Jewish Studies

The truth is that the university has been basically *Protestant*—though nonsectarian, liberal, and kindly disposed toward Jewish and Catholic as well as Hindu, Buddhist, and Moslem students and their religions. It was the Protestant vision which determined American university perspectives until the most recent past. That vision is, admittedly, broader and more mature than the Jewish or Roman Catholic equivalents. The New Testament and the history of Christianity are not systematically studied in any Jewish-sponsored university, in this country or in the State of Israel, except in relationship to the history of Judaism, whereas great attention has been paid at notable nonsectarian, Protestant-oriented universities to the Jewish tradition. Philip Ashby points out that the history of the history of religions in America cannot be separated from the history of Protestant theological education.[5] I think one may fairly add that the history of all forms of the study of religion in secular American universities can be written in terms of the history of cultural, if not religious, Protestantism. Nevertheless, it is hard to see how others, of different religious traditions or of secular orientation, have improved upon the Protestant record.

With the growing maturity of the history of religions, however, I see no alternative to both the inclusion of Jewish data in that discipline and the application of the issues and methods of that discipline to the study of Judaism. This, I suggest, is where Jewish studies have their most promising, best-integrated place within the university (outside of Near Eastern studies).

The history of religions, as I understand it, focuses upon the phenomena and the morphology of religions. It raises questions concerning the interpretation of the religious structures, including myths, ideas, theological attitudes, and rites and rituals, as means of perceiving reality, or organizing it, or construing it, used by men in diverse circumstances. The history of Judaism has already contributed considerable data to that inquiry, mainly through the researches of Erwin R. Goodenough and Gershom G. Scholem, each of whom has shown, the one with archeological, the other with mystical sources, the possibilities of relating Jewish religious data to the broader patterns discerned in other religious materials. Goodenough and Scholem were primarily historians of religion, secondarily historians of Judaism—though this ordering of interests affected not so much the result as the attitude, motivation, and focus of concern. Yet, although Goodenough and Scholem have contributed much, we are only just beginning to appreciate the potential uses to be made of Jewish data. When one considers, for example, that there is still no study of phenomenology of the rabbi, in his inseparable political, cultural, and religious roles, one wonders how the nature of religious leadership can as yet be fully and properly comprehended. The rabbi, no less than the shaman, ought to provide basic information about the nature of the religious virtuoso and what he represents to the minds of his followers.

More broadly, however, one may suppose that Judaism, which seems so remote and intellectual in its central value structure, is among the religions which have in past times laid the greatest stress upon the man-God in various forms, not only rabbinical but also messianic and, certainly within Hassidism, mediatorial. In its struggle against modern Christianity, modern Judaism has insisted that Jesus "could not possibly have been accepted by normative Jews as the Messiah" because the Jews could not have believed in a man-God or in a spiritual savior who was not a politician or a general. That denial, if correct, required the exclusion of Hassidism, only two generations behind the German Jewish scholars, of Frankism, three generations, and of Sabbateanism, four generations earlier. But it also excluded the possibility of comprehending the figure of the Talmudic rabbi himself.

A second interesting theme is surely the transmutation of religion with the desuetude of the ancient ways of perceiving reality. Descriptions of archaic or so-called primitive religions normally omit reference to modern or contemporary religious phenomena except among still archaic peoples. But the great question in the history (not merely philosophy) of religion must be: What happens when archaic reality comes to an end and modernism begins? It is one thing to regret, condemn, look back fondly or sadly. It is quite another simply to ignore the fact that something called, and calling itself, *religion* has persisted into modern times in various ways and forms and therefore requires study. I can think of no more interesting example of a religion in the throes of transmutation into the modern idiom, better documented, with more variations in time and space and subtleties of definition, than the history of modern Judaism.[6] I have mentioned only two issues within the history of religions which cannot, I think, be satisfactorily discussed without considerable attention to the history of Judaism. There are many others. It is therefore the history of *Judaism* which finds a most natural accommodation within the university curriculum. As a set of structures to be analyzed, and not as a set of theological (or other) propositions to be evaluated, Judaism becomes interesting in that setting. It is self-evident that the same principle holds for all religions, including Christianity. In particular, like the theologies of other traditions, the study of Jewish theology, *except* when examined from a comparative or morphological perspective by historians of religion, and *not* as a self-validating system, has no place in the university curriculum. It is where Judaism, among other religious traditions, provides evidence of a particularity in which broader categories or issues may be exemplified, or find expression, that Judaism becomes relevant to the curriculum of the university. I think it likely that Judaism will make its contribution toward the definition of larger structures of analysis. Eliade's work on archaic religions, Hinduism, and Christianity quite naturally provided him with particular data, out of which generalities or categories of analysis emerged. Given somewhat different data—a religion mostly without cathedral or temple for thousands of years, for example—he might well have raised different issues to begin with. Judaism focuses, in the terms of analysis proposed by Professor Jonathan Z. Smith, upon the following structures: holy people, the structure of election; Holy Land, the structure of sacred space, Zion and exile, Temple and synagogue; holy days, the structure of sacred time, the Sabbath, the feasts, the daily service; holy rites, structures of initiation; holy law and holy book, the cosmic law, personal piety, the law and interpretation; holy men, rabbi and student, the philosopher, the magician, the mystic, the Messiah, and the Hasid. These structures illustrate the viability of Eliade's basic scheme of analysis, but they also suggest ways in which particular Jewish data might modulate those categories.

I look forward, too, to the revivification of comparative studies of religions. In this the history of Judaism will both benefit and contribute. For example, taken in isolation, the rabbinical academy may be studied from antiquity to the present day, but without a significant awareness of what it really was, or what gave it its particular shape and method at a given time or place. When, however, one asks how the rabbinical school compared with the Hellenistic academy or the Christian monastery, how it functioned in society and in the faith, as contrasted with the equivalent structures in Manichaeism, Buddhism, or Islam, much new insight may result. And it was the rabbinical academy which was the apparently unique leadership-training institution of Judaism. Similarly, the comparison of the rabbi and the mandarin has yet to be undertaken. How much other central institutions—structures of belief or ritual or myth, and the like—may be illumined by contrast or comparison with those of other religious traditions we may only surmise. So while the history of Judaism has much to contribute to the history of religions, the issues of the wider field may raise wholly new questions, and provide quite novel perspectives, for the narrower one. Indeed, the richness of Scholem's perspectives derives in the end not from his grand study of Kabbalah, the science of which he himself founded, but rather from his ability to ask broader questions concerning the structure of Kabbalistic experience and thought.

We may turn, finally, to some issues confronting any aspect of the history of religions. First, what is to be the relationship between the historian of Judaism and the historian of religions? It is not unreasonable to expect the former to become familiar with the methods, issues, and ideas of the field as a whole and to see his task as part of a larger undertaking. But the other side of the coin is this: can a historian of religions make use of the history of Judaism without first becoming a specialist in Judaism? It is a painful and difficult question, for if, as I suggested above, Jewish studies must now depend to a significant extent upon the resources of Jewish, and not university, curricula, then how can a non-Jew hope to make a contribution to the history of Judaism or, through the history of Judaism, to the history of religions? On the one hand, it is difficult to conceive that anyone could acquire a genuine mastery of Judaism without a close study of the texts which for the most part preserve it. Judaism has few monuments outside of books, and the "native speakers" of the tradition, those who embody one or another aspect of the tradition in their own lives, are with few exceptions either not interested in addressing themselves to those outside the limited community of the faithful or incapable of doing so. Hence texts, almost alone, consti-

Modes of Jewish Studies

tute the available evidence. To read them, one must know Hebrew and know it well. And to read them well, one must have undergone a long apprenticeship in mastering texts which represent a fundamentally *oral* tradition that has been transcribed. Talmudic studies in particular cannot be mastered without a teacher or, better, several teachers in both the old and modern manners.

Can Judaism be studied by one who has no personal relationship to it? Why not! Many useful inquiries can be made by the historian of religions. First, since most of the major rabbinic texts of classical times exist in good English translations, the scholar who comes with paticular issues or questions in mind may well locate what he feels is relevant and proceed to restudy the classical text in the original. Second, and more important, the historian of religions should be able to depend upon the results of the scholarship of others—philologists, text critics, commentators, historians, historians of law, art, music, and theology, sociologist, and other scientists—and not have to repeat the processes which originally yielded their results. In every field of intellectual endeavor one customarily depends in some measure upon others, either predecessors or colleagues in cognate fields. Jewish learning does not present an arcane and remote exception. The contrary view, that the true scholar is only one who has gone through the traditional processes of learning in the traditional modes and then rejected them for modern scholarship, predominates in many circles of Jewish scholarship. It reveals the latent mandarinism of Jewish learning (itself a datum for the history of religions). The mastery of specific texts, mastered in ancient ways, through the old commentaries upon the old questions, constitutes the primary qualification for scholarship. What is important is not what one can do with what one knows, but what one has "been through," as if exposure to the texts magically transformed and therefore qualified the student. Modern scholarship adds a second qualification, namely, disenchantment with the old methods after such exposure to them. It is no less a magical view of learning, but one which elevates to a norm the experience of alienation.

The question of studying a religion not one's own generally depends upon the supposition that one's own religion plays a central part in one's capacity to comprehend some other. I do not see this as a serious classroom problem at the outset. Professor Jonathan Smith's syllabus opens with the words: "In this course, we will survey some of the basic religious structures of Judaism, using categories derived from the discipline of the History of Religions. Your task will be to try to interpret a representative sample of Jewish religious expressions—not in order to judge them as 'true' or 'false,' or to ask questions as to their contemporary or personal 'relevance'—but rather to strive to understand what they have meant and mean to a group who have expressed themselves, and the meaning of their existence, who have constructed and interpreted their world and their history through these religious myths, symbols, and rituals." In my view, that sentence partially lays to rest the ghost of "personal involvement." (But see below.)

This is not to say that the study of the history of Judaism is not likely to raise certain broader questions about the nature of religion or the "science" of religion. After the tasks of description, interpretation, and understanding have been undertaken, the further responsibility of reconstituting the data into the raw material for philosophy of religion has yet to be carried out. But I do not see how that work can be done in the narrow framework of the history of Judaism, as it is studied in the university classroom. Rather, it is to be done in two ways and for two different purposes: first, in the Jewish seminary, for theological purposes; and, second, in the philosophy of religion, for phenomenological purposes.

One can hardly overestimate, moreover, the importance *for* Jewish learning of the study of the history of Judaism within the context of the history of religions. Ashby quotes Kitagawa as follows:

> The expert in one religion must also be cognizant of the nature, history, and expressions of religion beyond the one religion he seeks to understand. Adequate understanding of one religion is seldom, if ever, achieved by knowledge about that religion only. The historian of religions needs to possess wide knowledge of his subject in its universal expressions if he is to fathom one religion in depth.[7]

So far, with the major exceptions of Scholem and Goodenough, historians of Judaism have not taken comparative approaches very seriously. It is true that they have conjectured about "influences" of one thing upon something else—for example, Iranian influences upon Qumran; but only rarely have they transcended such narrow, positivistic questions. Most scholars of Jewish subjects would, moreover, accept Kitagawa's statement if it were phrased in any terms other than religion. It is recognized that one must have command of several languages, literatures, histories, and cultures in order to study various aspects of the Jews or Judaica. Jewish scholarship was born in the age of positivism, however, and has remained ever since the last refuge of fundamentalist, naive, positivistic thinking. It has, therefore, not even bothered to apply its reductionist presuppositions to Judaism as a religion but, instead, has by and large ignored it from the start. So very little effort is devoted to the study of the history of Judaism that it is not even included in the curriculum of the Jewish Theological Seminary or in the programs of most other institutions of Jewish learning. No Jewish institution of higher learning here or overseas has a department of religious studies of any consequence. If it were possible, some scholars of Judaica would deny that Judaism has existed as a religion in any sense, regarding it only as a law, a culture or "civilization," a nation (people), or something—anything—other than a "religion," or religious tradition. Others will go so far as to deny that Judaism, if it is a religion, has had any theologies. An examination of the pages of Jewish scholarly journals will uncover remarkably few articles about Jewish religion, though there are a great many which contribute in some way to the study of Jewish religion. But those contributions take the form of intellectual or social history, philology, sociology, and textual criticism. The central contribution to the study of Judaism now emerging in the universities will be a methodology appropriate to the study of the history of Judaism joined with concern for that study.

We therefore have a provisional task at hand: to learn what are appropriate issues and methods and to bring these issues and methods to bear upon a rich and practically untouched, almost unknown religion. Since that religion has entered a new age in its history, with the general decay of premodern forms in the West, it should be clear that few Jews are in the situation of the Buddhist who comes to the West to study Buddhism. Similarly, since the effort to convert the Jews seems finally to be concluded, except as an eschatological hope to be left for the eschaton, Christians normally do not come to the study of Judaism in order to master the information necessary to undertake a mission to the Jews. Normally atheists are less bothered by the absurdities of Judaism than by those of Christianity, which impinge more readily upon their consciousness. One's personal emotional condition can play no role of consequence in the study of a religion which few in the West have held in its classical forms for at least a century. Accordingly, whatever engagement of feeling we find may be of two kinds. First, it may be similar to the engagement of the classicist or the antiquarian, namely, a fondness for the dead past and its glories. Since it is dead, one may speak of its glories. So far as it is alive—and in its many modulations Judaism is very much alive—one cannot yet know what these glories may be, or what they are not. But the history of Judaism extends backward in time far, far beyond the nineteenth century, to at least the destruction of the first Temple, and I see sufficient grounds for many far-reaching investigations long before "feelings" and "involvements" pose much difficulty. Since Eliade refers to problems of esthetics, it may be useful to draw an analogy from the study of the history of art. One may penetrate very deeply, I think, into the art of Rembrandt without for a single minute intending to paint in his fashion. One may similarly penetrate deeply into the understanding of Jewish religion on its own plane of reference, or on the plane of reference of religion as a phenomenon in human history, without intending to adopt that religion or any other. The "modernization" of Judaism, therefore, is what may make possible the study of its history.

Nonetheless, I think I err on the side of optimism. There is a second form of engagement of feeling not to be ignored or denied. The very involvement of Jewish scholars in the study of Judaism is bound to operate as a personal factor. For example, the influence of Yehezkel Kaufman's *History of the Religion of Israel* upon biblical scholars of Conservative Jewish origin cannot be explained entirely in terms of the persuasiveness of Kaufman's case, if only because he has made very little headway elsewhere. Kaufman supplies, rather, a peculiarly satisfying way for biblical scholarship in a supposedly modern form to coexist with a very traditional, indeed primitive, formulation of Jewish theology, especially for people who want to continue to study the Bible as revelation. Having abandoned the classical faith in the Pentateuch as revealed by God to Moses on Mt. Sinai, the Conservative Jewish scholar finds comfort in Kaufman's arguments leading to much the same faith, but on a much more positivistic basis, in the "Mosaic revolution" of monotheism within Israelite culture. It would, moreover, be a misunderstanding of the modernization of Judaism to suppose that modern Jews see themselves as discontinuous with the past. On the contrary, the very stuff of their modernism is the effort to restructure or re-form inherited, archaic beliefs, attitudes, and patterns. Whether this is quite selfconsciously undertaken, as in Reform and Conservative Judaism, or quite unselfconscious to begin with, as among so-called Orthodox and secular Jews, is not at issue here.

What is important is that the modern proceeds from the archaic, and their relationships are subtle and difficult to comprehend. Hence the Jewish scholar of Judaism, however secular or objective he may think himself, must still conscientiously attempt to meet Kitagawa's conditions, just as other historians of religion must, and for much the same reason: "First is a sympathetic understanding of religions other than one's own; second is an attitude of self-criticism, or even skepticism, about one's own religious background. And third is the 'scientific' temper."[8] In the beginning the Jewish historian of Judaism must see both himself and his enterprise as themselves constituting data in the modern history of Judaism. So, as elsewhere, the very act of scholarship affects what is under study.

Conclusion

The broad range of Jewish studies may contribute to the university curriculum at many points, but the particular point at which a specialist in Jewish studies most nearly approximates the university's needs is in the field of the history of Judaism. This is not to suggest that specialists in the Hebrew language and the study of Hebrew literature do not belong in departments of Near Eastern languages and literatures, for they do, even though before recent times Hebrew literature was hardly a Near Eastern creation at any single, significant stage in its history after the tenth century. Specialists in the sociology of the Jewish community may well make a noteworthy contribution to the social sciences. Specialists in a given period and locale of Jewish history obviously have their appropriate place in a history department, so long as they are adequately trained to make a contribution to the broader interests of that department. Specialists in medieval Jewish philosophy or in modern Jewish "thought" may join in the discussions of the history of philosophy, or even in modern philosophical discourse pursued in old-fashioned ways (where these still persist). But so far as Jewish studies cover an *area* by means of many *disciplines,* there can be no place for a department of Jewish studies, though a center involving disciplinary specialists of many kinds obviously would serve a useful purpose. And so far as a university offers a strong program in the study of religions, it is in *that* program that its primary appointment in Jewish studies should quite naturally find its place, but not to the exclusion of an appointment in Hebrew language and literature. Given the predominant content of those studies, I think this is the only appropriate way of handling the matter.

There is one final point to be made: the development of Jewish studies in universities must not be shaped to meet the parochial interests of the Jewish community, the synagogue, or Judaism. Jewish community groups have discovered that the future of the community is being decided upon the campus. They have therefore chosen to strengthen programs aimed at influencing the Jewish college student to come to an affirmative decision upon basic issues of Jewish identity and commitment. As chaplaincy, or Hillel programs, such efforts are wholly unobjectionable. It is, however, quite natural for Jewish community groups to look upon professors in the field of Jewish learning in general, and of the history of Judaism in particular, as allies in the "struggle." They are widely expected to continue in the classroom the advocacy of Judaism which begins in the synagogue schools and continues in the pulpit. Secular Jewish organizations, interested in recruiting future leaders for their fund-raising and other programs, similarly turn to the campus and therefore to the professor of Jewish studies, particularly when he is a Jew to begin with, for support. Jewish studies certainly belong in parochial settings as well as in universities. When in universities, however, neither such studies nor those responsible for pursuing them must be used for propagandistic purposes of any kind. It is not the duty of the professor of the history of Judaism, or of Hebrew, to take an interest in the state of the souls of students, whether Jewish or gentile. Our true task is impossible if we fail to see ourselves and our students as constituting data for the study of the history of Judaism. It is certainly not the task of any professor to serve other than university commitments. It may, therefore, be wise for universities to avoid dependence upon Jewish community funds in the creation and maintenance of programs in the field of Jewish learning. I am not suggesting that the Jewish community and synagogue are more dangerous as a pressure group than any other, but only that they are no less so. In any event, rabbis and others who have achieved considerable mastery of Jewish traditional learning are not, on that account alone, appropriate candidates for full or, more especially, part-time university posts, any more than are local priests or ministers. Nothing will so endanger the healthy development of Jewish learning in its various modes within the university as the exploitation of that development for other than strictly and narrowly defined university purposes.

Judaic studies, that is, the study of the history of Judaism, and Hebrew studies, the study of Hebrew language and literature, together belong within the university curriculum of the humanities, the latter to serve the interests not only of linguists or Semitists but also of students of religion. If, as G. E. von Grunebaum said, "a humanistic education will essay to evoke the widest possible range of responses to the stimuli of civilization,"[9] then within it the history of Judaism provides a number of important perspectives. It is the account of the development of a world religion from almost the very beginnings of human history up to the present day. It includes the most varied forms and expressions of that world religion, its organization into several sorts of political systems, its narrowing into essentially salvific forms, its broadening into a whole civilization (in Central and Eastern Europe), and then its renewed development in a series of complex and subtle responses to the modern situation. In the development of Judaism, foreign cultural traditions were absorbed, modified, eliminated, illustrating the processes of cultural interaction and transformation.[10] Finally, the history of Judaism contains a number of unifying elements, shared by other Western religions yet in some ways absolutely unique. Judaism is, as von Grunebaum said of Islam, "both close enough to the Western view of the world to be intellectually and emotionally understandable and sufficiently far removed from it to deepen, by contrast, the self-interpretation of the West."[11]

Notes

1 For a survey of the existing pattern, see Arnold J. Band, "Jewish Studies in American Liberal Arts Colleges and Universities," in *American Jewish Year Book*, 58, ed. Morris Fine, Milton Himmelfarb, and Martha Jelenko (New York and Philadelphia: Jewish Publication Society of America, 1966), pp. 3–30. Band compiled a list of 54 professors and 34 Hillel directors teaching courses at 92 American colleges and universities. Among the top graduate and undergraduate schools (41), Band found that what he calls "Judaics" are offered in the following departments:
Near Eastern studies (including Oriental studies, etc.)—14
Religious studies—12
Classics—4
Foreign languages (including modern languages, linguistics)—5
German—2
Jewish studies (or Hebrew studies)—2
English—1
Philosophy and religious studies—1
The field seems mostly divided between departments of Near Eastern or Oriental studies, which stress language and literature, and departments of religion.
2 See the very helpful comments of Raphael Loewe, "Defining Judaism: Some Ground-clearing," *Jewish Journal of Sociology* 7, no. 2 (1965): 153–75.
3 I am well aware that one- and multivolume histories of the Jews have been written. These are invariably highly theological (ideological), frequently homiletical treatises, in which given themes, such as the nobility of the Jews and the heartlessness of their (generally) Christian neighbors, the literary productivity ("culture") of the Jews and the benighted and narrow minds of their neighbors, and the like, are played upon. Before World War II such histories concluded at the climax of "the Enlightenment and Emancipation," which seemed then to be the happy ending of the long bloody story. Afterward, the State of Israel generally provided the dramatic conclusion for the narrative. I know of only one

exception to the rule that a comprehensive "history of the Jews" is bound to be of less than professional historical quality, and that is Salo W. Baron's *Social and Religious History of the Jews* 15 vols. (New York: Columbia University Press, 1952).

4 Of special interest in this connection are N. N. Glatzer, "Beginnings of Modern Jewish Studies," in *Studies in Nineteenth-Century Jewish Intellectual History*, ed. A. Altmann (Cambridge: Harvard University Press, 1964), pp. 27–45, and N. N. Glatzer, "Challenge to the Scholar: A Judaic View," in *Judaism* 11, no. 3 (1962): 210–20. I subscribe wholeheartedly to Professor Glatzer's theses in the latter article.

5 Philip Ashby, "The History of Religions," in *Religion*, ed. Paul Ramsey (Englewood Cliffs, N.J.: Prentice-Hall, 1965), pp. 1–49, passim.

6 I have tried to present one useful structure of interpretation of the history of modern Judaism in "From Theology to Ideology: The Transmutations of Judaism in Modern Times," in *Churches and States*, ed. K. H. Silvert (New York: American Universities Field Staff, 1967), pp. 13–48.

7 Ashby, "The History of Religions," p. 44.

8 Joseph M. Kitagawa, "The History of Religions in America," in *The History of Religions: Essays in Methodology*, ed. Mircea Eliade and Joseph M. Kitagawa (Chicago: University of Chicago Press, 1959), pp. 1–30. Quotation is on p. 15.

9 G. E. von Grunebaum, "Islam in a Humanistic Education," in *The Traditional Near East*, ed. J. Stewart-Robinson (Englewood Cliffs, N.J.: Prentice-Hall, 1966), pp. 36–68 (reprinted from *Journal of General Education* 4 [1949]: 12–31). Quotation is on p. 36.

10 Paraphrase of ibid., p. 37.

11 Ibid.

Part Two

Academic Disciplines and Jewish Learning

2. Here and Now

Prospects for Graduate Education

Jonathan Z. Smith

There seems to be a curious embarrassment with respect to the topic of graduate education. While many faculty are well-scarred veterans of long and elaborate discussions of general or departmental undergraduate curricula, most are rank amateurs when it comes to discussions of graduate education. To be sure, we sometimes fiddle with details, change the examination structure, work out possibilities for substitutions of languages. We are accustomed to worrying about employment for our students going out, and the number and quality of our students coming in. But it is rare that we discuss the enterprise as a whole, or call it into question.

At first glance this appears plausible, especially insofar as we continue to identify graduate education with the dissertation. In most academic convocations, there is a revealing difference in ceremonial formulae. The candidates for doctoral degrees are commended for having successfully completed an original piece of research which contributes to knowledge in a particular field; the candidates for bachelor degrees are commended for having successfully completed a program of studies prescribed by the faculty. Doctoral studies appear to result in a clear product—a monograph. Undergraduate studies are a process, a program. The former has a concrete and visible terminus; the latter, an artificial interruption. As long as we do not subject the doctoral formula to a set of rude questions, there is something self-evident about the tangible result of graduate studies.

So long as we focus on the dissertation, the kinds of educational issues often raised with respect to undergraduate programs seem carping, idiosyncratic, and irrelevant. A piece of work is a piece of work, nothing more needs to be said. The dissertation is self-justifying, complete in itself. In Johan Huizinga's formulation: "It is quite unnecessary for each monograph to justify itself. . . . An entity in the cosmos, it has within itself the same right to exist as every blackbird that sings and every cow that eats grass."[1]

From such a vantage point, the curriculum leading to the doctoral degree can be reduced to a "need-to-know" basis. The model of doctoral studies appears to be that of the tutorial or apprenticeship. The more general requirements seem to exist only as prolegomena to the act of focus, to the definition of the terminal task, or to serve as ancillaries to it.

While I suspect that I might get broad agreement on such a notion of graduate studies *sub specie dissertationis,* the burden of my argument in this essay will be against such a view, both with respect to the academy in general, and with respect to the study of religion in particular (the latter being the context I best understand for graduate studies in Judaism).

With respect to the academy, it would be my contention that the focus on the dissertation is, in far too many programs, irresponsible and unrealistic. Despite striking corporate and individual exceptions, the academy does not appear to be an enterprise of sustained scholarship. The bulk of productive, important, and ever-maturing research is done by a small minority. If we count only such research as achieves publication, the minority contracts even further. For example, it has been estimated that some ten percent of the faculty members in the United States are responsible for more than eighty-five percent of the scholarly publications. I take one implication of this to be that, in more instances than we may care to admit, a student is directed in his or her dissertation by a faculty member whose only significant act of research was his or her dissertation.

A significant number of faculty members are not competent to direct the kind of sustained research that results in the monographic dissertation; a good many graduate students are not yet ready and certainly most are not well trained for the kind of sustained research that results in the monographic dissertation. As a result, the faculty member and the graduate student appear to enter into a covenant of banality with the following sorts of results.

In far too many dissertations from a variety of institutions that it has been my lot to read, the initial chapter is often devoted to a review of previous scholarship that witnesses to little more than a capacity to use, indifferently, a modest number of bibliographical tools. Rarely is there critical evaluation. The principle appears to be, if it was said, it is worth noting. Rarely is there the capacity to account for the various results of one's predecessors, whether in terms of some wider history of ideas or of disciplines, or some sociology of knowledge. Figures are allowed to cohabit the page who would assassinate each other if placed together in a room, so varied are their presuppositions, methods, and interests. This the author of the dissertation has failed to detect, having only read the "relevant" paragraph or page—if, indeed, the reference was not cribbed. In such a chapter, a motley list of sorts may have been achieved, but not history, not the winning of a useful historical-critical perspective.

Turning next to the body of this putative dissertation, one rapidly discovers why the more leisurely and discursive term "dissertation" has come to replace the more combative and assertive term "thesis." For there is rarely an argument, at least rarely an argument conducted by any logical or dialectical rules. No clarity on the roles of definitions, classifications, and explanations—the central building blocks of academic discourse. No sense of what constitutes an objection, of "what counts." No precision in stipulating a domain. No painful and argued decisions of choice. All is equal. Everything is of equivalent gravity. All that is required is for it to have been "there."

Alongside of this inability to argue and to accept responsibility for decisions of inclusion and exclusion, there is often a bland nodding to authority. The rule seems to be: do not say something yourself if a quotation, no matter how dubious the source, can be found. And, thanks to modern xerography, make the quotation as long as possible, and leave the reader free to choose for himself what portion he finds relevant or interesting. (If all else fails, the rule appears to continue, state in a footnote, "it is interesting to note . . . ," but never specify in what the interest lies.)

The "concluding" chapter is precisely not that. It does not venture any conclusions, at least in a form that might advance research. Rather it reviews and summarizes the previous chapters, and frequently promises subsequent work which will be (alas) more of the same. There are no proposals as to the implications of the research for the definition of the scholarly field. No predictions as to the necessary entailments for others' work. No specifications as to the degree to which the results achieved, the questions asked, the methods employed, the data chosen are to be taken as exemplary of a wider range of topics, or what modifications might have to be made if they were to be elsewhere applied. This, I suspect, is due to the fact that the series of intellectual tasks and objectives just proposed imply a trained self-consciousness that is, more often than not, utterly lacking. There has been no explicit training in such matters. All has been left to the accidents of osmosis and mimesis. Instead, there is an overwhelming sense of relief to the final chapter—on the part of student, professor, and reader—at having achieved the end of a period of time and a task which will be looked back upon with frustration and distaste.

In presenting such a composite dissertation, I have, of course, exaggerated. But not by so great a degree as to allow the illusion of comfort. The picture is bleak, but its bleakness, given the present state of the academy, was predictable. In the undeniable truism of the cybernetic sage: "Garbage in, garbage out."

The reader will have noted that, in so caricaturing this imaginary but all-too-typical dissertation, I have provided, as well, an implicit formulation of a generic description of what ought to be the content of graduate studies. That is to say, whatever else they learn, graduate students should be exposed to their disciplinary past in such a way as to learn the art of critical evaluation and to gain the ability to account for this past in terms of a broadly based historical consciousness. They must learn the context of their second-order tradition as well as they have mastered the primary texts, and the difficult art of evaluating each in terms of the other as well as in terms of historical perspectives and intellectual principles. They should learn, through explicit attention to rules and by the careful study of examples, the crafts of argument and dialectics, the art of making things count and of determining what counts, as well as more philosophical issues relative to the types and status of definitions, taxonomies, and explanations. They should be capable of stipulating why their chosen data are exemplary in terms of clearly stated, well-formulated issues central to their academic discipline. And they should be taught ways of "cost accounting" for the decisions of choice and interpretation that they make.

Such concerns, and there are others which might have equal claim for attention, are not the domain of any particular discipline or field of study. *They are what constitutes an endeavor as academic.* They constitute the elements of a general education at the graduate level. If the dissertation is to continue to be perceived as the culminating point of graduate studies, the students must learn, along with the appropriate field-specific skills, the generic arts of arguing a thesis and specifying its implications. And they must learn these arts through courses explicitly devoted to this end. We cannot continue our present fixation on the dissertation without a proper curriculum which balances both the generic claims of the academy and the more specific claims of a given field of inquiry.[2]

The focus on the dissertation, and the concomitant reduction of the curriculum to a "need-to-know" basis, have had a further negative effect on the academy. For all the weight placed on the enterprise of sustained (and, frequently, solitary) scholarship in graduate programs, the majority of their faculty, and the majority of their students, teach and will teach heavily in undergraduate programs. This is all but unacknowledged in the formalities of graduate education.

The fact remains that, despite much talk about the relationship of teaching to research, the recognition that the majority of the positions in the future will be in undergraduate programs, and the widespread employment of graduate students in instructional roles, there is little explicit attention to teaching in most graduate programs. What occurs, with heroic exceptions, seems to take place largely by accident or as a result of an uncommon, and ultimately countereducational, faith in imitation and trial and error. I would think that it would be possible to design teaching requirements as a part of the Ph.D—at the very least, to require the submission of a proposed syllabus for a course of the student's design with a written rationale for the various elements and pedagogic strategies, or the preparation of a series of critical reviews of the major undergraduate textbooks in one's field of interest, with the development of seminars or colloquia in support of these. Such requirements, alongside the more usual modes of in-service training, especially if the latter included analyzing the pedagogics and performance of a course as well as its subject matter, would be a modest beginning. I would hope for a time when it would be as routine a matter to deny a degree to a student who failed a teaching requirement as it would to one who failed some linguistic or special-area examination.

Thus far, I have focused on the teleology of graduate studies: the dissertation and the teaching. But this is not what is, for me, at stake. Through such a focus I hoped to suggest that what we most lack in so many instances is a *conception of a graduate program*, a graduate curriculum. To put this another way, we appear to do best, and to have expended most effort, at the beginning and end of graduate instruction, at the crafting of the introductory course and at the intense mentor relationship. What we lack is a graceful *middle range*. In program after program, in field after field, I find no rationale for what is offered between a student's first course and the moment when he or she has fulfilled all course requirements. The variety of courses may be interesting, they may be well taught, they may be responsibly undertaken. But they do not cohere, they are rarely cumulative, they often seem ignorant of one another. They reflect well the varied, individual interests of the faculty, but they do not set forth some corporate understanding of a discipline or field, they reflect no institutional judgment. They appear to initiate into idiosyncratic styles, not into a sense of a profession or craft. What structures there are most closely resemble undergraduate distribution requirements and may be subjected to the same criticism: the students are being asked, unaided, to integrate what the faculty will not.

If we are to continue as an academy, we cannot remain so careless of the large range of courses which stretch in between the introduction and the dissertation. It is here that our students spend the majority of their time; it is here that the intellectual and professional context of one's future work is formed; it is here that a discipline is forged; and, for these reasons, it is here that the curricular discussions and corporate decisions of the future will have to be focused.

Against this general background, the particular matter of religious studies at the graduate level may be seen more clearly. Indeed, the matters raised above become more pressing because of the peculiar history of religious studies within the academy. For most of western educational history, religious studies were carried on within theological faculties, within seminaries, where the appropriate emphasis was on the study and transmission of the received tradition by adherents of that tradition, where the appropriate goal was the training of a learned clergy. This was changed, in theory, on October 1, 1877, when the Dutch Universities Act separated the theological faculties at the four state universities from the Dutch Reformed Church. For the first time in western academic history, there were established two parallel possibilities for the study of religion: a humanistic mode within the secular academy which might have as its object of thought some *generic conception of religion;* and a theological course of study within the seminary largely devoted to one of the religions. The original draft of the legislation had proposed to call the new department the faculty of religious sciences, but, after much debate and compromise, the older title, faculty of theology, was retained. Nevertheless, dogmatics and practical theology, the central core of a Protestant theological education, were removed from the curriculum, henceforth to be taught only in the seminaries. Their place was taken by a new program in history of religions which was assumed to be more "neutral and scientific."

France followed soon after. In 1884, the French ministry of education abolished the state Catholic theological faculties and, a year later, replaced them (with a sense of Gallic irony, in the very same building) by the "fifth section of religious sciences" as part of the École Pratique des Hautes Études. Religious studies were thus placed alongside the other four sections: mathematics, the physical sciences, the biological sciences, and the historical-philological sciences. The minister of public education charged the new faculty: "We do not wish to see the cultivation of polemics, but of critical research. We wish to see the examination of texts, not the discussion of dogmas."[3]

In 1904, the University of Manchester, which was unusual among British universities in being nondenominational, in applying no confessional tests to either students or faculty, established a new theological faculty which taught both theological subjects and comparative religions, but which excluded courses in systematic theology and the history of Christian doctrine.

Few other European countries followed this pattern. In most of Europe, religious studies were a part of the divine sciences; the degree was a theological degree.

In the United States, until some twenty years ago, a sequential pattern prevailed. That is to say, a doctoral degree in religious studies (whether from a seminary or a university) had, more often than not, the prerequisite of a bachelor of divinity degree from a seminary.

With few exceptions, it was not until the rise of graduate programs in state universities, a development which largely followed the 1963 United States Supreme Court *School District of Abington v. Schempp* decision, that the parallel course of study, instituted a century earlier in Holland, became a widespread possibility in this country.

I have rehearsed this well-known history in order to make two points. First, *the debates over the nature of the academic study of religion have rarely been substantive; they have been largely political and tactical.* That is to say, they have been informed by concerns not so much indigenous to the academy as appropriate to legislative bodies and legal questions of the relationship between church and state. Second, until recently, *the graduate study of religion was preceded, in the typical student's career, by a course of postbaccalaureate professional study within a theological faculty.*

Let me address this second point first, because it is crucial for the understanding of the present dilemma of religious studies within the academy, dominated as it is by Protestant concerns and models. It is this second point as well which exacerbates, for religious studies, the more generic problems sketched above with respect to graduate education.

The issue was put with precision by Claude Welch in his 1971 comprehensive report *Graduate Education in Religion: A Critical Appraisal* (a report which, by the way, despite the harsh criticism with which it was greeted in some quarters, wears exceedingly well).

What is to take the place of the theological degree [i.e., the B.D.] as the base on which advanced studies in religion are built? A distinctive feature of the tradition of graduate education in religion is that there were important common bases. The traditional route to the doctoral degree for Protestant, Catholic and Jew alike, was through the seminary curriculum. This is still true of the majority of students in Ph.D. studies . . . [but] increasing numbers of students are going directly into graduate work in religion with indifference or even disdain for study in the professional theological schools. The new trend poses a problem, however, because whatever the merits or demerits of the professional orientation of the seminary curriculum, the traditional route did provide both depth and breadth within the limits of a major religious tradition on which it was possible to build real specialization. There was, in other words, a common base or core of study. . . . But, if the movement to by-pass the theological degree continues to grow—and it will—and if "religious studies" is to be defined as other than strictly Catholic studies or Jewish studies or Buddhist studies or Hindu studies, the situation is genuinely critical. Either we fall into a chaos of simply unrelated investigations, in which no one can finally talk to anyone else, or we search for new patterns of coherence.[4]

    The academic study of religion is not taught in most public high schools. The graduate study of religion cannot rely on coherent undergraduate religion programs to replace the lost though limited coherence of the theological degree. If one surveys the various undergraduate curricula and course syllabi, in most cases there is little that is common beyond some components adapted from the seminaries. If one surveys the textbooks, there is overwhelming evidence for religious studies' lack of a "second-order" tradition.[5] Each textbook that strives for generality represents either an idiosyncratic attempt at incoherent synthesis (e.g., the texts authored by Fred Streng) or an encyclopedia of trivia (e.g., the shockingly widely used text by John Noss). There is no guarantee that any topic or figure treated in one textbook will be even mentioned in another which claims to introduce the same field. All is ad hoc. All appears to be improvisation.

    What we have not faced as a profession is that our "second-order" tradition at the graduate level was, for more than a century, provided by the B.D. or its equivalent. Having had the luxury of this common core upon which to build a graduate curriculum, we irresponsibly failed to provide its equivalent once this prerequisite was jettisoned. Having had the additional luxury of this negative contrast against which to position the academic study of religion, we have now lost our "common enemy." (These problems are made more difficult by the introduction of non-western religions into the curriculum, taught by individuals largely trained in philological or area studies programs which appear to lack any principles of coherence beyond the ability to decipher a non-Roman alphabet.)

The bachelor's degree cannot provide this coherence. The undergraduate programs will not be brought into order except by the models provided and the teachers trained by the graduate faculties. But these have been unwilling to work at the challenge of providing a new core.

There is an additional reason for this failure of nerve within religious studies. To develop this I must reiterate a previous point. Religious studies have almost never defined themselves in a substantive manner; rather, they have been preoccupied with politics and tactics.

The issues raised by the large literature on the academic study of religion since the late 1950s, when religious studies programs within state universities first became possible, have been largely those of *legitimacy*. The putative separation of church and state, as well as the concomitant suspicion that religion could not be addressed academically, made these matters urgent. Hence the endless discussion of questions of objectivity and subjectivity, of the descriptive and the normative, and other such matters that would be incomprehensible apart from a political situation in which legitimacy is conferred not by the academy as a result of public scholarly achievement and utility, but rather by legalistic formulations that license the teaching "about" religion but not the teaching "of" religion (to crudely paraphrase Mr. Justice Goldberg's historic, but equally crude, opinion).

Even our more overtly substantive discussions are suspect as being, in fact, political and tactical. One does not have to be a Marxist to discern some economic substrate beneath our ideological formulations. For example, in the expansionist 1960s, we argued that religion was an irreducible, sui generis phenomenon. Translation: a separate department of religion was required. In the contractive late 1970s and early 1980s, we have argued that religious studies are uniquely "polymethodical" (or, as one colleague facetiously suggests, drawing on the old folk tune, we "sing polymethodoodle all the day"). Translation: an ill-willed provost cannot dispense with religious studies, because he can't find them. They are intercalated with the humanities and social sciences.

Of more gravity, if we were to develop a consensus on the academic study of religion such that a proper curriculum could be generated, we would have to recognize that behind all the questions of alleged substance (as well as those of law and politics) lies a set of unexamined, certainly Christian, chiefly Protestant, presuppositions which have guaranteed that the majority of the religious phenomena of mankind will remain forever un-understandable. In so many respects, seen from the perspective of a general study of religion, Protestantism is an exception which requires explanation; it cannot be used as a model for explanation.

The preoccupation with the categories of belief and faith, the primacy of individual experience, the distinction between a sphere of religion and a sphere of civility, the derogation of ritual, the primacy of the text—these, and almost every other category developed internally within the field of religious studies, are dependent upon and incomprehensible without peculiarly Protestant presuppositions. Nor, when we go "outside," is there much difference. That we appropriate sociologies with categories such as charisma and routinization, church and sect; that we find models in the allegedly anthropological (but, in fact, covertly theological) tradition of Parsons, Geertz, and Bellah, are only to meet these same Protestant presuppositions but slightly translated into another language. Furthermore, by being "religious" rather than theological, these old theological agenda are cut off from all responsibility to a community consensus and to a received tradition. Within the "secular" academy, they are free to be irresponsible. An individual theology is a contradiction in terms, yet it is precisely this which, in the academy, often passes for and provides the agendum of some theory of religion.

It is for these reasons that I am eager to join in the discussion represented by the essays in this volume. I have no particular interest in the study of Judaism, except insofar as it can contribute to the enterprise of developing the general study of religion. The categories that may be developed with respect to the Jewish materials may be distant enough to call into question the traditional categories of religious studies, yet related enough for discourse rather than mere juxtaposition to be possible. I am not interested in a Jewish theory of religion (whatever that would be), or in categories so crafted as to apply only to Jewish phenomena (however they be defined). But I am concerned with the possibility of developing a critique of our present presuppositions. And here the study of Judaism in the academy might be of some modest aid. As I have written in another context, "The interest of the student of religion in Judaism cannot depend on apologetic, historical or demographic reasons. That is to say, the interest in Judaism for the imagination of religion cannot be merely because it is 'there,' because it has played some role in our collective invention of western civilization, or because some students of religion happen to be Jews. Rather it is because of the peculiar position of Judaism within the larger framework of the imagining of western religion: close, yet distant; similar, yet strange; 'occidental,' yet 'oriental'; common place, yet exotic. This tension between the familiar and the unfamiliar, at the very heart of the imagining of Judaism, has enormous cognitive power. It invites, it requires, comparison. Judaism is foreign enough to most students of religion for comparison and interpretation to be necessary; it is close enough for comparison and interpretation to be possible. By virtue of its tensive situation between the near and the far, Judaism provides an important test case for central methodological issues such as definition and comparison besides illuminating the larger areas of imagination, self-consciousness and choice crucial to the academic study of religion."[6] It is only when such central issues and larger questions are corporately and explicitly addressed that we may begin to develop a core and a curriculum for graduate studies and gain explanatory power for the more particular investigations represented by the dissertation. If not now, when? If not here, where?

Notes

1 J. Huizinga, "The Task of Cultural History," in *Men and Ideas: Essays by Johan Huizinga*, ed. J. S. Holmes and H. van Marle (New York, 1959), p. 22.

2 As long as present practice holds in the hiring of faculty, I have little

hope for the alteration of the notion that graduate study is a preparation for the dissertation. But I applaud proposals such as the one from a department at a major research university to keep the traditional monographic dissertation in place for those who elect it, but to offer an alternative for those who do not. Analyzing the kinds of tasks performed by the scholar-teacher in the contemporary academy, this proposal suggested three requirements which might be fulfilled in lieu of the dissertation: (1) the preparation of a scholarly article on a focused topic that would be accepted by a refereed journal; (2) the preparation of a long, generalizing chapter on a genre or historical period of the sort that might appear in a standard multivolumed reference work (such as the *Cambridge History*); and (3) the presentation of a lecture open to the general public as well as to the academy on some topic of interest and concern growing out of the student's work. I am interested in recommending not so much the details as the impulse which lay behind this proposal—the recognition of a variety of roles in today's academic profession, not all of which are well served or tested for by the traditional monographic dissertation.

3 E. J. Sharpe, *Comparative Religion: A History* (London, 1975), p. 122.
4 C. Welch, *Graduate Education in Religion: A Critical Proposal* (Missoula, Mont., 1971), pp. 21–22.
5 I owe the formulation of religious studies' lack of a "second-order tradition" to an unpublished paper by Walter Capps of the University of California, Santa Barbara.
6 J. Z. Smith, *Imagining Religion* (Chicago, 1982), p. xii.

3. Judaism within the Disciplines of Religious Studies

Perspectives on Graduate Education

Jacob Neusner

Religions flourish nearly everywhere. Everyone has opinions about them. Given the claims of religions and the data adduced in their behalf, we may hardly find it surprising that every opinion about a religion demands a solemn hearing. It is the one academic field in which one can make things up as one goes along and then expect (and get) serious attention to this morning's truth. But as everyone knows, while nonsense is nonsense, the history of nonsense is scholarship. So too are the sociology, economics, politics, literature, languages, philosophy, theology, architecture, dance, music, art, psychology, philology, archeology, and geography of nonsense. All the logoi of humanistic and social learning severally and jointly take up, but do not exhaust, the matter of religion too. Furthermore, there is always place for comparison of one person's nonsense to another's, and of one tribe's religion to another's. Now when we claim to study Judaisms, the religions of the Jewish people, we propose to describe, analyze, and interpret the complex of the world view and way of life characteristic of the social group, meant to make sense of Jews' lives, and their life together, under the aspect of heaven. Just as, when we study religion, we study nearly everything about nearly everybody, so when we allege that we study Judaism, we can hardly leave out anything about the Jews. Under these capacious circumstances, what sort of learning is possible, and to what end?

To answer these questions, let us make the leap across the bottomless abyss, that is, the catalogue of the humanities and social sciences I recited a moment ago by which in theory one *might* study religion. Rather, we must try to reach the side of reality, that is, how religion today *is* studied. For there is no point in attempting, through totally abstract theorizing, to reflect on how a field is shaped and transmitted in graduate school. We gain nothing by idle speculation on what the field might do to cover the subject entrusted to it. As the protean force in humanity's civilization in nearly all of its forms and expressions, religion is everywhere and everything. It is what unites, what makes sense of the whole. But who can encompass the whole anyhow? Still, that is not how we study religion, or why we take up the disciplines of religious studies. So with a regretful glance upward, into the heavens of free and rapid movement over vast landscapes of learning, we lower our eyes to earth, slowly to see the contours of a few acres of the university's campus, indeed, to trudge across the one or two plots of furrowed soil where we actually work.

Let me begin with a statement of what I think we study when, in universities, within the humanistic disciplines, we study religion. It derives from an unpublished address of Jonathan Z. Smith, delivered May 20, 1982:

> What we study when we study religion is one mode of man's characteristic effort at constructing worlds of meaning. . . . What we study . . . is the passion and drama of man discovering and expressing the truth of what it is to be human. Religion is the quest, within the bounds of the human, historical condition, for the power to manipulate and negotiate, to imagine one's situation, so as to have "space" in which meaningfully to dwell. It is the power to construct a "domain" in such a way as to guarantee the conviction that one's existence matters. Religion is thus a distinctive mode of human creativity. . . . What we study when we

study religion is the variety of attempts to map . . . and inhabit positions of power through the uses of myths, rituals, and experiences of transformation.

To this I need add only that if we hope to understand the Jewish people and the things it has made and done, we have to study Judaism in the setting and disciplines of religious studies. These can help us understand how the smallest and weakest of peoples has managed to endure and overcome and claim to discover for itself the reason why.

We now take up two questions. First, what do people actually do when they study religion? Second, what, in that context, do they do when they study about Judaism?

The first question governs the answers to the second. We begin with the simple observation that the study of religion is not only as old as civilization, it also is as new as our own university world since World War II. From the moment someone made scratches of bison on the walls of caves, generations have been taught the meaning of the glyphs. The walls of the caves are caked in the soot of many lamps, kindled over centuries by people coming to learn the tradition of the scratchings. The study of religion is not solely the study of the bison. It also is sifting through the soot on the walls and ceiling round about. There is more soot than scratching.

Religions have never lost their critical place in both the formation of the lives of social groups and the explanation of the life of each member of each social group. Throughout time insiders always are the ones to study religions: each one his own tribe's religion, each one her own life as explained by that religion. But the twin and inseparable notions (1) that there is such a thing as religion, not merely religions, and (2) that nonparticipants may learn something worth knowing about other peoples' religions and also about religion as a general thing—those two notions really are new. They were scarcely known before the Enlightenment (unless we include Spinoza), little celebrated since then. The science of religion takes place mainly in the scholar's study. If we ask ourselves where we can find discourse *about* religion—as distinct from (learned) expressions *of* diverse religions, one by one—we have to find our way to the libraries and classrooms of a handful of scholars. For while, as I said, everyone talks within or about religions, only a few people have tried to draw the infinite phenomena of religions together and so speak about religion. Fewer still have made the effort to talk intelligibly, to generalize not only responsibly (that is, informedly) but also in an interesting way.

Where do people study about religion? The cultural and social conditions that make possible the exercise of detached inquiry into religion as a universal fact of humanity present themselves principally in universities. Here people claim to wish to speak together, on the basis of solid learning, about significant issues. Yet even here, the universities have to be of a particular order: secular, Western, mostly American. That is, the study of religion is a uniquely Western phenomenon, flourishing in particular under secular auspices on the one side, or under the auspices of religious people attempting to address a secular, or at least an alien, world on the other. Since World War II, Western, and, in particular, English-speaking and French-speaking universities have proved most hospitable to departments of religious studies, as distinct from theological studies of religions. (*Religionsgeschichte* in Germany and Austria is scarcely a ghost of its former glory.) The reason is that the countries of the West proposed after World War II to take up discourse with all the countries of the world, shaping an international vision of learning as part of a larger perception of culture and of national standing in an international matrix.

If we wish to consider the state of religious studies in the world today, we ask simply who attends international congresses on the study of religions—as distinct from meetings on the study of particular religions, or particular holy books of particular religions. There will be many Americans and Canadians, Australians and British; some French; a paltry handful of Spanish, Italians, and Latin Americans; a fair number of Scandinavians; some Germans; and nobody else. Except for an occasional Japanese, an Asian is a curiosity, a specimen, a mere holy man. To state matters still more clearly, if we ask where we find the study of religion within philosophical faculties (in the European sense) or within departments devoted solely to religious studies, as distinct from theological faculties, seminaries, and divinity schools, the answer is this: there are many such departments in America and Canada, two or three in all of Britain, and a handful in France and Germany.

Everywhere else, religious people study their respective religions;

that is, not religion, but theology defines the field. Accordingly, in Germany, Holland, Britain, Scandinavia, and elsewhere, Christianity is studied in theology faculties, and everything else is covered as philology or within philosophy faculties, for example, Judaism or Buddhism or the nonliterate religions. So there is theological and philological study of religions, but little religious study of religion. When religions other than Christianity find their way into theological curricula, moreover, the interests of future ministers define what is studied. (So, in Germany, for instance, *Judaistik* is treated as an aspect of New Testament studies at least as commonly as it is treated in its own context.)

This long recitation of what I understand to be the cultural and social conditions under which the study of religion becomes possible yields a simple fact: religious studies constitute a discipline (or a set of closely related disciplines) principally in the English-speaking world, and mainly in North America. The neutral, humanistic, or social-scientific study of religion, as distinct from the theological study of religions, comes about, in particular, where churches or synagogues or mosques or temples stand essentially separate from universities and governments alike. In this country we understand that the state is not to intervene in the practice or study of religions or to support one particular church, or even all synagogues, churches, mosques, and temples, all together. We therefore have created that condition of autonomy for religions that makes possible the interest of ordinary folk in making sense of the phenomenon of religion, hence, also, in studying the phenomena of religions held by other people. That is the main point: the interest in learning about religions other than one's own religion. The academic study of religions and religion serves as a barometer for a society's breadth of vision, range of curiosity, and interest in the other. *The science of religion, properly carried out, is the study of the other, the science, par excellence, of how to study the other.*

Let us take up the question of what people do when they study religion. The question is readily dissected into its principal parts: (1) who teaches (2) what (3) to whom? and (4) where does this teaching take place?

To start with the fourth question: The academic study of religion found its home in departments of religion or religious studies only in

Perspectives on Graduate Education 51

the decades after World War II. The earliest generation of professors of religious studies normally had divinity degrees; many had gotten their doctorates either in divinity schools or in philosophy, working therefore in the sacred scriptures of Western religions, on the one side, or in philosophy of religion, on the other. Later on, when the faculties expanded to include Eastern religions, the professors tended to come out of philological disciplines, from Sanskrit into Indian religions, from Arabic into Islam, or from Hebrew and Semitics, or Talmudic or other Jewish texts, into Judaism. So, in the main, the earlier generation generally held its degrees in either philosophy, theology, or philology; there was no degree mainly in religion. What they taught, quite naturally, was what they knew, that is to say, a particular religious tradition. So the curricula of the field began in the transfer of the Protestant seminary curriculum to the college. In the nature of things, later on, when Catholics arrived on the scene, they tended to take courses in something called Catholicism, Jews in Judaism, and everyone in Bible, church history, and philosophy of religion, the Protestant subjects. In the later sixties, the Eastern religions found their audience, as natural to them (people supposed) as was Judaism to the Jews. It is only a mild caricature to describe the study of Eastern religions as Buddhist monks teaching mystical, mystified Americans the Sanskrit word for cow.

Today it would be a gross exaggeration to say that people in general study religion. But we have passed the point at which diverse "peoples' or churches study their particular religions. Likewise, we no longer deal with a generation of professors most of whom who hold, also, divinity or rabbinical degrees or their equivalents. But the faculty and students who make up the field also focus, quite naturally, on what they find familiar. As at the outset, the majority of religion students today tend to pursue their roots, or things so presented as to look like roots. Accordingly, to take the case at hand, it is not correct to allege that, in the case of Judaism, we have rabbis teaching Judaism to Jews. But it is not entirely wrong either.

My earlier account of the field ought to have left some puzzlement with the "what" of the question, Who teaches *what* to whom? For we do not yet teach religion, though we are trying to teach more than religions. We are presently attempting to discover how the study of a given religion may serve, for the humanities, to exemplify matters of common concern and general intelligibility. The work is under way, but progress is modest, and the workers, few indeed. We also have yet to frame methods distinctive to the study of religion. So far we have managed to take over methods of inquiry established in other areas and make use of them. But in adapting them, we have not yet made them our own. Accordingly, from philosophy we derive philosophy of religion, from sociology and anthropology analytical methods of sociology and anthropology of religion. From philology we learn to read our particular texts; and from history we learn to portray our distinctive historical and social subjects, religions at some moments in their histories. But there is as yet no field theory of religious studies, in which all of the discrete and diverse methods by which we study religions are so reframed as to constitute a well-defined method for studying religion. Whether or not such a field theory is possible and how, if it is, it will reshape our approach to the study of diverse religions are not questions with which I can deal.

Rather, I turn directly to the primary question at hand, the study of Judaism within the disciplines of religious studies. Once we have in mind the present state of the study of religions and religion, we realize that, for Judaism as for other religious traditions, we stand at the most primitive stages of the shaping of an academic field. Just as there is no clearly defined method in religious studies, but only the adaptations of diverse methods shaped elsewhere, the same is so for Judaism in the setting of religious studies. We accommodate our data to other people's questions. The ambiguity of studying not religions one by one but religions as they exemplify religion strikes us as beyond resolution. So is it the case with Judaism. What do we do when we study Judaism not in the setting defined by Judaism alone? If, like all other religious traditions, Judaism is asked to speak intelligibly to a common program of inquiry, then what is that Judaism that is asked to speak? And whence the definition of the shared agenda of learning? We select data to accommodate a program shaped out of data other than ours.

Clearly, in framing these questions, we move very far from the already familiar and explored territory of Jewish learning. Jewish learning by definition is particular, distinctive to Jews. It rarely asks itself how it addresses a common program of inquiry and speaks to the general interests of undifferentiated humanity. Pursued in Jewish schools, Jewish studies scarcely can be expected to frame discourse of general intelligibility. It follows that the academic study of religion is not only an essentially new field in the humanities and social sciences. Its fundamental attributes of mind lack all precedent in Jewish learning.

We may hardly be surprised that the Israeli universities' programs in Jewish studies make no provision whatsoever for religious study of Judaism, in the terms in which I have described the academic study of religions. Nor should the absence of the disciplines of religious studies from the curricula of American and European Jewish institutions of higher learning, whether universities or rabbinical schools, elicit surprise. Both settings cultivate monopolies of learning, protected by high walls of indifference. The two streams of Jewish learning, traditional and so-called *wissenschaftlich*, have not yet flowed over this new territory, for (to continue the metaphor) high dams stand in the way. For the traditional curriculum the notion of standing apart from "Torah," describing it in a context in which "Torah" by definition is not unique but subject to comparison with other peoples' Torahs, is unthinkable. The claim of uniqueness presents a high wall indeed against all humanistic inquiry. For the new curriculum of *Wissenschaft des Judenthums*, with its interest in history, philology, and philosophy, the commitment to militant positivism closes the way to the study of the intangibles of the spirit that comprise religion. The materialist or positivist ideology of blood, peoplehood, and history, offered by the scholarship of *Wissenschaft des Judenthums* to the modernized sector of the Jewish people, not much different from the theology of divine revelation of a unique Torah to a unique people, makes no provision whatsoever for the inquiry into the common ephemera of humanity on which the academic study of religion is based. For the mentality of positivism, religion is difficult to grasp and study. We know what people *do* because they are religious. It is harder to say what religion *is*. For the framers and continuators of modernized Jewish scholarship, therefore, Judaism as religion is scarcely accessible.

In the present context, we again remember that "religion" exists only in the mind and imagination of the scholar of religion. Not "religion" but only religions flourish in the "real" world of nations and churches. The scholar of religion, as I said, emerges from a quite particular set of circumstances. To Judaism these circumstances are new. So we must not be surprised that, for Judaism, as for so many other religions, the academic study of religion remains alien to the intellectual life of the faith. Disciplines able to affirm the particularities of the faith, such as history and philology, dealing with the one people and its one language, work very well in Jewish learning. They affirm history, blood, and peoplehood, all in exquisitely learned detail. Those disciplines by definition transcendent of particularities, framed to ask general questions about particular things, do not work at all in Jewish learning. They rapidly dispose of claims of uniqueness in which parochial learning rests.

Now the absence from the field of Jewish learning of the disciplines of religious studies need not produce dismay. What is dismaying is that when we look at religious studies where they come to full expression in organized departments, we find only modest achievements. Forgive me now for asking some embarrassing questions of the disciplines of religious studies. But it is past time.

First, has the discipline produced a common curriculum, based on a firm consensus on what we think education in the discipline should accomplish?

Second, does scholarship in the discipline follow a program of inquiry, so that there is perceptible progress in the investigation of long-term questions?

Third, are there criteria by which achievement is recognized and triviality and pretention properly labeled?

To answer the first question, a student of the curricula of undergraduate departments will have to use a very fine magnifying glass indeed to uncover among diverse departments the marks of common educational theories of the subject. People teach pretty much whatever they want about different religious traditions and call the consequent conglomerate "the study of religion." But it is not. It is only studies of religions.

Second, having spent my life as a scholar, more than two decades, in the field of religious studies, I state simply that people are still arguing about the same things they discussed twenty years ago. They are worse than the Bourbons: they have forgotten everything they ever heard from others, and remember only the positions they originally held.

Third, people in religious studies attain very high rank on the basis of publications and other evidences of scholarly achievement that in history or biology or engineering would be regarded as paltry. (In this regard Jewish studies are equally self-indulgent.) People holding named chairs in major universities float onward and upward on the inflated balloons of their published dissertations. Issues of theological doctrine or personality govern appointments that in other disciplines are determined by attainments in scholarship and teaching.

In times past religious Jews were suspect in religious studies. Today, by contrast, wearing a head covering indicates mastery of Judaism, without regard to what, if anything, is inside the head. Piety and saintliness ornament our lives together. They do not constitute qualifications for scholarship and they do not serve as indications of learning. Indeed, these days they may suggest the very opposite. So the academic study of religion from one perspective appears to be an afflicted field that has gone from birth to old age without bothering to make the promises of youth and without rejoicing in the fulfillment of maturity.

Why indeed should practitioners of the field of Jewish learning venture into so blighted a field, plant seeds in soil capable of producing only so scrawny a crop? No defense will serve for the academic labor-saving devices at home nearly everywhere in departments of religious studies. If the discipline of religious studies deserves admission into the sanctum of Jewish learning, it is because of what from that discipline people learn in Jewish studies. Insofar as Jewish learning takes up the Jews' heritage to nearly the present time, it is a fundamentally religious statement. If we study what Jews have thought and felt and been outside of the framework of religion, we miss the point. The Jews have regarded their society as special ("chosen"), themselves as holy, their books as "Torah" (revealed by God). So the right questions to raise to describe these things have to be questions about holy people, holy books, holy faith. We want to know what these assertions teach about those who make them. Insofar as the Jews have seen themselves within the heightened mythic framework evoked by the word "Israel," they constitute a problem in particular for the study of religion. And the very insistence, by Jews, upon the deep meaning of their collective life, upon the uniqueness of their history, an insistence common for so-called secular, as much as religious, Jews, marks the life of the Jews as a phenomenon for the inquiry of scholars of religion.

Let me state matters negatively. Even though, through philology, we understand every word of a text, and, through history, we know just what happened in the event or time to which the text testifies, we still do not understand that text. A religious text serves not merely the purposes of philology or history. It demands its proper place as a statement of religion. Read as anything but a statement of religion, it is misunderstood. Accordingly, despite the primitive condition of religious studies as presently practiced, the discipline-in-the-making known as religious studies does promise for Jewish learning what has not yet been attained. That is the capacity to describe, analyze, and interpret, in its own terms, without embarrassment and without vulgar reductionism, the inner life of "Israel," the Jewish people. When we emerge from both the theology of the Torah myth, and the secular apologetic of history, blood, and peoplehood, we must ask ourselves how to take seriously, in its own terms, the heritage of humanity that is the Jewish people. The answer is to treat that heritage as a statement, in terms of heaven, of what it means to be human here on earth. Insofar as the bulk of Israel's heritage turns out, in the comparative context of the heritage of other nations, to be religious, it is to be studied as we study other religions, in the setting of the humanities and the social sciences.

This account of the place of Judaism within the disciplines of religious studies has been protracted; the following perspective of graduate education will be brief. That is the right proportion. For the way we define a graduate degree expresses our theory of the field and tells what it is important to know, and to be able to do, within that field. When we teach our doctoral students and shape their curriculum, as we do, we define the field for the coming generation. We select and hand on what we find of worth, not only in the little that we know, but also, and especially, in the *way* in which we do things. So a theory of the field of the doctorate comes prior to a practical expression of that theory in doctoral studies.

How shall we prepare young people to enter this new field, this nonfield, this field lacking a curriculum, a research program, a coherent body of standards—this pathetic but necessary field of religious studies? How, further, is someone to be prepared to study the religion of the Jewish people, when that religion encompasses almost everything that makes Jews distinctive? Who in the end can ever become competent? Who can claim to describe, analyze, and interpret the complex of world views, ways of life, and social groups that have been and are the data of Judaism? What does it mean to study nearly everything about nearly everybody who was ever or now is a Jew? It cannot be done. It is not worth doing—not in these terms.

In the protean universe of religious studies, absurdly encompassing the whole and trying to see it in its totality, we must set our eyes on some one thing, not on everything. Likewise in the religious study of Judaism, we must make choices. Imperfect vision defines our condition. The alternative is not more eyes (or omniscience) but blindness. If detail is all we ever see, then we shall have to learn to see the whole in one of the parts, the universe in a grain of sand.

We therefore tote up our list of incompetences, the things about which we must know something, so as to see a detail of the whole, but can never know enough, and never in ample context and completely. We speak of obvious things. Scholars have to be able to read the texts that are their sources, so graduate students must be taught to read. Scholars have to formulate suggestive and interesting questions of these sources, so graduate students must be shown what it means to ask. Scholars have to be able to speak intelligibly, therefore to a common program of inquiry and in a common language of discourse, shared with other thoughtful people. So graduate students must be taught to think and write.

To read *what,* to ask *what,* to think and write about *what*—these are matters of mere detail. To be sure, life is in the details. But once framed, our curriculum serves a variety of subjects. In the field of religious studies, our mode of inquiry is always the same. We ask specific questions, aiming at answers of general intelligibility. We want to explain, in terms commonly understood, experiences people claim to be unique and private. We aim at transcending the otherness of the other. To do so we seek to make the particular into something exemplary, an example of what is general. In the end, if we are to study religion, beyond religions, that is what we have to do.

How we teach these things emerges from our distinctive task. A field lacking a well-framed method cannot be taught, it can only be learned. The best we can do in graduate education is guide students' programs of learning, helping them to make themselves into professors and scholars. Insofar as education is the work of socialization, we do educate—but in that sense alone. For when we teach texts, we do not teach the study of religion, and when we teach generalizations about those texts (or other sources of the data of religions and religion), we transmit what is scarcely subject to testing or even replication. The state of the art so limits us that, in generalizing, we hand on impressions, opinions framed as fact, guesswork dressed up as insight. So we do not have much to teach, though our students have a great deal to learn. What we can offer is only the model of how to work, the insight of an informed vision and an experienced eye, what we learn in failing and disappointment. We can teach them to keep trying. For that purpose, we have to define graduate education in terms of an apprenticeship.

That is to say, we best teach when we do our work before the eyes of our students, who then stand in relationship to us as do disciples to a master or apprentices to a craftsman. So we teach by doing and correcting, and our students learn by doing and receiving correction. All we teach is our criticism of our own work. We teach by correcting what the students do, revising and forever recasting our own work alongside theirs. At the outset therefore students have to take up the task on their own, because, as I said, in a field lacking developed methods, we learn through trial and error. What this means in practice, as far as I am concerned, is that the dissertation starts on the first day of graduate studies and continues to nearly the end. Doing the dissertation, if the work is well defined, forms the center of the student's graduate education. In order to do that one work, the student discovers the need to know many things. Ever-widening circles of learning, an ever-expanding frame of discourse—these naturally derive from that well-crafted project at the center. The dissertation serves as the stone cast into the still pool.

The apprentice copies what the master does, but then uses what is learned to make something quite beyond imagining. In recommending the apprenticeship as a model for graduate education in this discipline and field of learning, I stand on solid precedent. First, as everyone knows, the classical texts of Judaism themselves were framed and handed on through the relationship of master and disciple. Second, less familiar in this setting is the fact that, in the great traditions of art, the apprentice both copies the distinctive technique of the master and makes it his own. The study of religion today is an art, so it can be learned as described in this passage by James A. Michener ("On Integrity in Journalism," *U.S. News and World Report*, May 4, 1981, p. 79):

> Young people learn their profession, whatever it may be, by studying the best work of their predecessors. I shall never forget the delight with which I saw a great painting done by Giovanni Bellini which had been copied by his pupil Titian. Rubens had learned by copying Titian to see what his secrets were, and Delacroix had copied Rubens. Van Gogh did a marvelous adaptation of Delacroix, so that we had five of our greatest, most distinctive painters, men of the most intense personal style and integrity, striving to learn what good artists of the past had accomplished.

Let me conclude with some general observations. Graduate education, though demanding and difficult, decides the future of learning. In the brief interval of three or four years of seminars, we turn informed people into scholars and teachers. To outsiders to the work, it seems as if we confer a mere union card; we contrive an obstacle course to keep ourselves occupied; it is a ritual of initiation into a profession. But to those of us who define and do the work, it is the work that matters. For we can say what we think marks success and failure.

The result of this work of teaching is, alas, public. When our students become teachers in their own right, with a mature vision of their responsibility to the generations to come in the classroom, then in their success we have succeeded. But if our students emerge as mere technocrats, well trained to purvey information, but not to convey understanding and appreciation for the subject that is ours and theirs, we have failed. When our students leave us, first book in hand, rich in plans for a second and third and fourth, then we have succeeded. For we have given not merely a degree but a program of inquiry, a life's work, a reason for knowing, a dream, a vision, a hope, a quest. But if our students see the dissertation as drudgery, the writing of a book as an unattainable height, not worth scaling, we have failed. We have let loose upon the future a time-server, a robot of information, a dead soul, yet another bore to validate the common meaning imputed to the awful word "academic." When we reflect that doctoral studies in America reach back scarcely a hundred years, and in the West not much more than a half-century more (beginning with von Humboldt in Germany), we realize that we Jews have more to teach than to learn. For our tradition of educating highly selected experts, teachers of truth, authorities able to make reliable judgments in some one thing goes back in a continuous line for nearly twenty centuries. The lessons to be learned for graduate studies from the master-disciple relationship constitute our richest contribution to graduate studies in America. Among these, let me conclude by specifying three. First, graduate education for the doctorate must be accomplished through crafted and considered relationships between each student and each teacher. It cannot be done in numbers. Second, graduate education depends upon respect for the learning of the master. Experience and tenacious, long-term work, for the humanities at least, must govern. The graduate teacher serves to criticize, not to praise; to educate, not to validate what is already known. There is no room for the autodidact in graduate school. Third, the Judaic tradition declares that learning differs from mere opinion. Everyone's vote does not count equally. The American tradition of egalitarianism, to be prized in many things, does not belong in learning (or in university governance). Some people do know more than others. Everyone's opinion is not worth the same as everyone else's. The Judaic encounter with ongoing intellectual life teaches one lesson above all: respect for knowing, for the one who knows, for the thing known.

What we do is new and old. It is unprecedented for Judaism to come under study outside of the schools of the Jewish people, whether religious or secular. It is a moment with few precedents for Judaism to attract the friendly, but essentially noncommittal, interest of people who are not Jews, who have no intention of becoming Jews, and who also are not obsessed with the Jews and Judaism. Since the locus of study is fresh, the focus of learning likewise shifts. New sorts of people are asking new questions. They address their questions in such a way as to make everything appear as though no one had ever seen it before. And the truth is, in this fresh way no one has.

But under study, we need hardly remind ourselves, is the age-old people of Israel, with its ancient writings, its established points of insistence and concern, and its hoary traditions of wisdom and of how and why learning is to be acquired. How then shall we determine whether what we do in new ways is worthy of the ancient setting in which we do it, the antique and ever-renewed intellectual tradition of Israel? I think one criterion is this: if whatever we see presents us with a fresh and surprising vision, we are faithful to our own age. If we try to be mindful of the greatness inhering in the things on which we work, so that, were we to meet the creators of it all, we should not have reason to be ashamed before them, then we may also be worthy of the thing we learn. True, we cannot claim each morning to invent the wheel. But we also may not deny that every day the world begins anew, and we with it.

4. Contemporary Jewish Studies in the Social Sciences Analytic Themes and Doctoral Studies

Calvin Goldscheider &

Alan S. Zuckerman

Introduction

A focus on doctoral programs in contemporary Jewish studies is exceptional in two ways. First, contemporary Jewish studies have not been an integrated mode of teaching and research in programs within Jewish studies in particular, and within the university in general. Second, when modern Jewish studies have been taught at the graduate level, they have been frequently located within departments associated with the social sciences. The particular selection of research issue, topic, course of study, and method of analysis concerned with contemporary Jewish subjects has been idiosyncratic and individualistic. A topic is interesting, a professor is interested, so research is pursued. There is little logic to the choice, no organizing principles, no sustained research focus, little coordination and cumulation of effort. Modern Jewish studies in the academy have been the accident of person and subject; they have been the stepchild of both Jewish studies and of the social sciences. In no American

Jewish Studies in the Social Sciences 63

university is there a systematic doctoral program focusing on contemporary Jews and their communities.

This state of affairs reflects general factors such as the legitimacy of the social science enterprise in Jewish studies, the growth of particular fields of specialization within the social sciences, the narrowness of disciplinary perspectives, and the specialized tools and techniques of social science. The fundamental issue has been who controls academic territories and intellectual domains. The absence of social science perspectives in Jewish studies programs in America reflects the politics of the academy, not theoretical concerns. We shall leave it to the historians and sociologists of ideas to agonize over the whys. However interesting, we want to pursue other issues here.

We *assume* that social science theories, methods, and evidence are legitimate in the university. We *assert* that they are not trivial; they are fundamental to understanding human society in all of its manifestations. Social science is not the only perspective, but it is a viable and legitimate one. It can be applied systematically to all societies, at all points in time. Some have done it for the biblical period, others for periods of the Mishnah and Talmud; still others have applied social science perspectives to other distant times and places. We and our social science colleagues use it for studying contemporary Jewries and their communities.

The underdeveloped state of contemporary Jewish studies does not reflect an absence of research materials or scholarly efforts. In the past decade, there has been an avalanche of studies—unprecedented in history—of Jews in various communities and societies. Little of this research is tied to general questions of theory and method. While some bemoan the state of dissertations in their fields (see Jonathan Z. Smith's essay in this volume), we have no doubt that we could match our mediocrities with theirs.

The growth in the number of studies focusing on contemporary Jewish issues, in conjunction with their theoretical and methodological underdevelopment, requires us to identify the major themes of the field. What is "modern" about modern Jewish studies? What is "Jewish" about contemporary Jewish studies? How do we separate modern Jewish studies from contemporary Jewish history? Is contemporary Jewish studies the continuing of Jewish history into the modern era? Is "contemporary" the moving present against its immediate past?

We do not want to draw a precise line between social science and modern Jewish studies, on the one hand, and contemporary Jewish history and history, on the other. There are clear intersections, as the hybrids social history, demographic history, historical sociology, and historical demography attest. Indeed, much of the especially creative work in the social sciences addresses issues connected with history, and historical work has outlined social-cultural-political-economic issues. Nor are the sources of historical and social science data so different; often the methodological and analytic techniques are similar. Certainly, the history that focuses on quantitative methods (and not only intellectual history or the history of ideas) uses advanced statistical techniques. Both social science and history employ theories, models, and explanations. Often these are less explicit in history, whereas in social science they are more clearly articulated. Historians tend to focus on details; social scientists usually look for overall patterns. But that contrast is not quite fair. It is partly a matter of style and emphasis; partly a matter of different goals of generalization and detail examined.

Without sharpening the differences, let us suggest how we can contribute analytically and systematically to understanding the past and present from different perspectives. And even within the field of social science there is an enormous range of emphasis and style, of theory and method. Within our own areas of expertise—sociology, demography, and political science—there is an enormous range. While we have reservations about how much we can influence the theories, methods, selection of issues, and modes of analysis of those outside our disciplines, we are convinced that programs which expose students to different views, perspectives, frameworks (as well as different substantive materials) are more challenging and exciting than those which are confined to one discipline or perspective.

In dealing with contemporary Jewish studies, the historian might be concerned first and foremost about defining the period. When does the modern era begin? When do we date the onset of modernity? Social scientists are less concerned about dating starting points in time than about focusing on processes. We want to direct most of our reflections on outlining the major processes, or analytic themes in the study of contemporary Jews. These analytic themes guide our understanding of the fundamental issues of Jews and their communities in the past century. It has been argued that religious studies have never been defined in a substantive manner (Smith, this volume); neither have contemporary Jewish studies. Before we can address issues of doctoral programs, of research and publishing, we need to know what are the central issues we are studying. Clearly, we cannot organize our teaching and research, except on a random basis, without an orientation to the whole. We need a picture in which to fit the various research parts so that our students of the next generation may build toward a grander synthesis.

Analytic Themes in Contemporary Jewish Studies

What are the major analytic issues in the study of contemporary Jews and their communities? A clearly articulated set of questions addresses broad issues relevant to the study of whole societies and communities within them. They are the first steps beyond random and idiosyncratic research toward a vision of the broader enterprise. Although these analytic themes are elementary in the social sciences, they have never been systematically addressed to modern Jewish society and politics.[1]

The master theme of contemporary social science is the analysis of the transformations of societies and the variety of groups within them as a result of modernization. Industrialization, urbanization, mobilization, secularization, and other changes are key elements. New structures and values, new institutions, ways of behaving and thinking, new jobs, residences, political movements, cultures, and ideologies, as well as new sources of conflict, competition, and inequalities have emerged in the modern era. Our master question is: What has been the impact of these transformations on the Jews? How has the modernization of the societies in which Jews lived affected them? How have Jewish communities responded to the sweep of modernization? With the dissolution of the older bases of cohesion, have new communal bonds and associational ties linked Jews with each other? What types of Jewish *Gesellschaft* have emerged out of the Jewish *Gemeinschaft?* What are the bases of solidarity, in the Durkheimian sense, as Jews and their communities were transformed by modernization?

Hence, our fundamental analytic issue focuses on changes over time and their effects on the Jews. We are concerned not with all change, but those particular kinds of changes associated with modernization. Many of our analytic concerns are linked to this basic issue. Many of our questions are variations, elaborations, and specifications around this major theme.

For example, we are interested in variation over geographic and political space. Here the concern is with Jewish differences among nations. The degree to which Jews in one country differ from Jews in another relates first and foremost to how and why the countries vary. Rates, levels, and the timing of modernization among places are major factors accounting for national variations among Jews. Differences between French and Russian Jews in the nineteenth century must first be traced to the broader differences between French and Russian societies. Beyond these differences are those that reflect the particular features of the Jewish community. Differences in the population size of Jewish communities, the strength of their institutions, and the legal constraints imposed by governments are important considerations.

The examination of Jewish community variations also addresses questions of interdependence. This may take two forms. First, we need to investigate links among units within countries. In particular, we study the relationships between local, regional, and national institutions. At times, such ties are asymmetrical, with core areas (for example, urban, metropolitan places) dominating peripheral areas. The links between core and periphery extend to interdependence among nations. Relationships between Jews in their national homeland and diaspora Jews can be examined in this context. Linkages between Jews in East and West Europe, between Europe and America require investigation. In particular, we need to know how these links are formed, how they change over time, and how they respond to the forces of modernization. It should be noted that we do not frame these links in the ideological context of Jewish peoplehood. We need not assume the wholeness of the Jewish people (over space or in history) to analyze the changing bonds among Jews in various places.

Jewish heterogeneity extends along other axes as well. These include social class, wealth, power, and socioeconomic variations (particularly education, occupation, and income), residential groupings within countries (regional patterns as well as rural, urban, suburban residence), and differences by religious denomination and ethnic origin. These variations highlight the differential impact of modernization on segments and sectors of the Jewish community and raise questions about how these variations among Jews parallel similar variations in the broader society.

The changing links of interdependence suggested by the variations among nations and communities have parallels in the internal heterogeneity among Jews within nations. In turn, these raise additional questions about convergence in modernization. Over time, do these Jewish interdependencies, cross-nationally and intranationally, create greater similarities among Jews? Do differences among Jewish communities narrow in the diffusion associated with modernization? How do these interdependencies create conflict and competition among Jews?

Issues of diffusion and convergence extend to another set of contrasts. The master theme of how Jews are affected by modernization deals directly with how Jews differ from non-Jews. A central problem in understanding modern Jewish society and politics is Jewish exceptionalism. If Jews differ systematically from other ethnic and religious groups, how are the differences to be interpreted? Are values and life-styles responsible for the differences? Are the structural factors of occupational concentration, educational attainment, and residential patterns the keys to why Jews differ from non-Jews? And do contacts between Jews and gentiles reduce differences? Are convergences between Jews and non-Jews similar to convergences among Jews? Does the diffusion of modernity neutralize the structural and cultural determinants of Jewish exceptionalism? These questions relate to communities as well as to individuals; to convergences and divergences in modernization; to the diminution of conflict, competition, and inequalities with modernization or to their accentuation.

These issues of modernization revolve around changes over time, heterogeneity, and exceptionalism. They apply to Jews and their communities as they apply to total societies and other ethnic and minority groups. There are, however, particularly Jewish issues of modernization, which are of critical importance in exploring modern Jewish society and politics. They relate to Judaism, anti-Semitism, and the internal organization of the Jewish community.

In the modernization of Jews, their religion is transformed. The normative centrality of Judaism declines. As the old order changes, so do the institutions legitimating that order. As religion changes and is redefined, new forms of communal identification emerge. How these changes evolve, what become the bases of the new forms of Jewish cohesion, and how communal consensus emerges in modernization are key issues. Moreover, the transformation from religious centrality to ethnic diversity poses the fundamental concern for Jewish continuities and discontinuities at the individual and community levels.

A second particular feature of an analysis of Jewish society and politics in the modern era relates specifically to anti-Semitism and to discrimination in general. How important are the attitudes, policies, and ideologies of governments and non-Jews in understanding the transformation of Jews? Does Jewish continuity reflect the unacceptability of Jews by non-Jews? Does discrimination increase or decrease in the process of modernization? How are political anti-Semitism and discrimination related to economic competition, conflict, and inequality? More specifically, how do political anti-Semitism and the Holocaust relate to each other and to Jewish continuity, on the one hand, and modernization, on the other?

The changing internal structure of the Jewish community is the final area of analytic concern. The organization of the Jewish community, its institutions and polity, is transformed in modernization. How and why the internal structure changed require analysis. In particular, are ideological factors the primary sources of growth, expansion, and contraction of the Jewish organizational pattern? How does competition among Jewish organizations and between Jewish and general institutions shape the emergence of and change in political and social institutions?

These issues are complex and interrelated. They are the fundamental concerns of social science. All focus on comparisons—over time, among groups, areas, communities. Systematic and multiple comparisons among Jews and between Jews and non-Jews are necessary in order to move beyond description.[2] The emphasis is upon behavior and characteristics of Jews and their communities. The study of elites, ideas, norms, and values is important, but it does not substitute for studying the behavior of the masses and the characteristics of their communities. The elite is not a cross section of the community; norms and values do not equal behavior. We must move beyond the study of the ideas of elites to the behavior of the whole society. We must place ideas in their social, economic, political, and cultural contexts and place elites in the body of the total community. Elite ideas are not the determinants of mass behavior or of even the behavior of the elites.

We need to ask the right questions and bring to bear on them empirical evidence. While we are concerned about the reliability and validity of the evidence, our thrust should be broader, our picture grander. We must focus on the patterns, knowing that perhaps some small segments are still unknown and others are known imperfectly. Nevertheless, as social scientists we emphasize the methodological links between theory and the empirical data. We synthesize systematically and theoretically the available evidence on the Jews.

Clearly our orientation suggests that an understanding of Jewish history and general social science is necessary but not sufficient for the task at hand. We need as well to place the study of Jewish society and politics in the contexts of ethnic and other minorities, general political movements, and other religions. Comparing Jews with others and others with Jews are the only ways to clarify these analytic issues.

Theoretical Frameworks in Contemporary Jewish Studies

To understand contemporary Jewish politics and society we need a comparative-historical framework. The enormous transformation of Jews in modernization touched every facet of their lives and institutions. We require a program of study which reflects the complexities of that transformation. We argue against historians who see the evolution of Jewish communities in various countries solely as products of their internal workings, the elite Jewish leadership, and the responses of non-Jews (or anti-Jewish attitudes). We disagree with social scientists who see ideological-cultural factors as the primary determinants of social change. Our position is that to understand the modernization of Jewish communities, we must examine the broader social and political contexts within which these changes occurred, to focus on the total Jewish community and not just the elite subgroups, and to see ideological and cultural factors as responses and consequences of social and political structural changes. Thus we focus on the modernization of Jewish communities in the same way as we might investigate the transformation of total societies. We examine the antecedent conditions, expansion, differentiation, mobility, conflicts, and competitions generated by modernization along with secularization, urbanization, segregation, and class formations. The questions are indeed the same (sharper perhaps); the unit of analysis is different.

More precisely, we ask how modernization affects Jewish continuity. What happens to Jews (as well as other groups defined by cultural, ascriptive, or political lines) as the forms of group cohesion are disrupted by modernization? Do minority, religious, and ethnic groups assimilate (i.e., disappear) as their bases of cohesion change? Do they melt into the new society and polity? Do they build alternative bases of continuity? Do new communal bonds emerge? Do conflict and polarization occur within the ethnic group?

Some theoretical models argue that systems of social organization based on religion and ethnicity are poorly adapted to the requirements of modernity. The spread of a national economy and bureaucracy entails universalistic criteria which cut across ethnic statuses. Ethnic attachments are replaced by social class and purely political cleavages.[3] The maintenance of ethnic cultural forms is partially an attempt to preserve a backward life style. If modernization means progress, ethnic continuity implies resistance to change. While there may be some ethnic remnants who are less affected by modernization, time and institutions (e.g., education) minimize their differences.

Ethnic persistence, therefore, is viewed as an aberration, a cultural lag, an unexpected feature of modernity to be explained away. Some have qualified the theory to argue that the presence of ethnic groups is based on selective political interests, cultural consensus, or external constraints such as discrimination and racism, or reflects nostalgic cultural traits of no depth or consequence.[4] The fundamental argument remains: Modernization leads to ethnic demise, except under particular or temporary conditions.

Another model places ethnicity in the context of exploitation, maintained by racism and discrimination. It analyzes ethnic groups via the concepts of power and control in the framework of "internal colonialism."[5] Modernization is spatially and socially uneven; initial advantage is crystallized and new advantaged groups are created. Conflict heightens ethnic cohesion. Exploitation and control over resources are the major sources of ethnic continuity.

This argument postulates that ethnicity equals disadvantage, particularly economic deprivation. In extreme form, ethnicity is viewed as epiphenomenal. It is not ethnicity per se but economic class conflict which is the core of ethnic continuity. The *overlap* between ethnicity and social class is, therefore, critical. This is referred to as the cultural division of labor, "a system of stratification in which objective cultural distinctions are superimposed upon class lines."[6] It is tied to territorial constraints related to core-periphery groups: "The core collectivity practices discrimination against the culturally distinct peoples who have been forced on less accessible inferior lands."[7]

The state subsequently reinforces the cultural division of labor. Institutionalized racism and discrimination through policies of differential access to schools, the military, jobs, and housing emerge. The overlap between residential and occupational concentrations gives a decisive advantage to the development of ethnic rather than class solidarity. The persistence of ethnicity is directly related to the continuation of the cultural division of labor. Intergroup contact strengthens ethnicity. Ethnic solidarity resembles class consciousness. The greater the inequality, the greater the cohesiveness.[8]

Both theories predict the eventual demise of ethnic groups. Either ethnicity is a temporary lag, a consequence of the absence of complete diffusion and convergence, or it is class based. When modernization is complete or when class inequalities are eliminated, ethnic groups will disappear.

There is yet another and we think more cogent view. It argues that inequality is not a necessary condition for ethnic continuity. As socioeconomic development diffuses over a territory, social groups become more homogeneous and the cultural division of labor erodes. The distribution of economic opportunities becomes more similar among core and peripheral groups. As competition among social groups for the same occupations, statuses, and economic rewards increases, new forms of ethnic solidarity emerge.[9] Furthermore, changes in the technology of industrial production and residential concentration, as well as common occupational patterns and ethnic organizations, produce and strengthen the continuity of ethnic groups. Each serves as a basis for ethnic cohesion. The more bases present, the stronger the cohesion.[10]

In this view, ethnicity is neither an ascribed nor a transitional characteristic. It is a continuous not a discrete variable. It emerges in the modern world and is not the cultural legacy of the past or a fixed primordial quality.[11]

This argument suggests further that ethnicity may be reinforced by a cultural division of labor. At the same time, that division does not necessarily imply disadvantage or economic deprivation. Ethnic inequalities are one route to ethnic cohesion; competition is another path.[12] In addition, the conjunction of ethnicity and occupation, as well as social and cultural organizations, political movements, and family and kin networks, is also a source of ethnic cohesion. These reinforce bonds of friendship and marriage, and, consequently, ethnic solidarity. When ethnicity does not involve economic disadvantage or competition, these institutional bases and social networks may still persist. Hence, even in the absence of a clear ethnic division of labor, ethnic solidarity may be found. Furthermore, international links between groups may heighten ethnic awareness and cohesion. They may take a variety of forms, including threats to the continuity of related ethnic groups in a national homeland or in other countries. Modern technology and communications have facilitated the broader links among ethnic groups beyond national boundaries. There are, therefore, a variety of bases of ethnic cohesion in the modern world.

The analysis of contemporary Jewish society and politics draws on these perspectives. Clearly, the prediction of assimilation is confounded by Jewish continuity in the contemporary world. Similarly, economic disadvantage cannot be a necessary basis for Jewish survival. Jews have not always been deprived or exploited economically. There are a variety of sources for Jewish continuity, comparatively and historically.

The analysis of modern Jewish society and politics elucidates general themes of the modernization of ethnic groups. At the same time, the study of general processes of ethnic modernization clarifies issues

Jewish Studies in the Social Sciences

of Jewish continuity and transformation. Jews, unlike other groups, were located in a variety of places within those areas of Europe which experienced the initial thrusts and subsequent intensities of modernization. They were concentrated as well in areas of later modernization in Eastern Europe under different regimes. Immigration brought them to America, the first new nation and the most modernized society. Other movements led Jews to a national homeland, where nation building and rapid modernization have been conspicuous features.

The comparative analysis of Jewish communities over the past century facilitates the examination of a wide range of conditions of modernization, at different time periods, and for different areas. At the same time, the mode of analysis helps clarify the patterns of change and continuity that have affected the Jews during the past one hundred years.

Studying and Teaching Contemporary Jewish Studies

What do these issues and research upon them tell us about how we should study them and how to educate the next generation to study them? Given these analytic concerns, it is depressing to review how contemporary Jewish studies are taught and researched in the university. Contemporary Jewish studies are composed largely of undergraduate and graduate service courses. They tend to relate to the Jewish identity of students, current events, and the Jewish community. The courses most conspicuous on campus deal with the Holocaust, Israeli society, and American Jews. They tend to be service courses for the university and for Jewish studies programs and do not focus on research methodologies. They cover substantive themes, not theoretical-analytic issues. Most are limited to one country with almost no systematic comparisons. Survey courses tend to deal with the details of modern Jewish history with no framework of analysis, cumulative theory and methodology, or obvious points of extension. Many do not fit into the regular program of study within social science departments and are "university" courses or located within a humanities-based department or program.

We are not calling for interdisciplinary programs in modern Jewish studies. Most such programs would end up multi- (not inter-) disciplinary. We suggest that instead of treating contemporary Jewish studies solely as a service to Jewish studies, we should treat Jewish studies as a service to social science programs on Jews. These should be primarily located in social science departments.

Jewish studies, it has been argued, are continuous with humanistic studies in universities.[13] We add that contemporary Jewish studies are continuous with the social sciences in universities.

One of the few discussions of contemporary Jewish studies in American universities suggested:

> We must remember that if Jewish studies in the American university are to have a vital future it will be because they fulfill a need which the young Jew feels. Thus the push to the study of Judaica must originate in the desire to explore personal identity. It follows then that the future of Jewish studies in the American university will be abortive if they move too far in the direction of becoming a pure and impersonal science.
>
> Given this impetus for the study of Judaica, the need for contemporary Jewish studies will become evident: in order to plumb his identity the young Jew will not only have to be familiar with the Jewish classics and the history of his remote ancestors, but he will have to study himself and his immediate forebears. . . .
> Without such concern modern Jewish scholarship will be neither modern nor Jewish.[14]

But contemporary Jewish studies that are modern and Jewish in that parochial sense will not be social science scholarship and will have no place in the academy.

Is a program of contemporary Jewish studies possible in the university? What should be its form? A doctoral program in contemporary Jewish studies would require a mastery of one of the disciplines of social science, not names, dates, and places in modern Jewish history. The student must study sociology, political science, anthropology, or economics and master the theoretical issues and methods of analysis of that discipline. In turn, the general theoretical and methodological tools would be applied to the analysis of contemporary Jewries. The student's goal (and that of the program) would be to contribute both to general theoretical questions and to the understanding of Jews in the modern period. Analyses of any one case are of interest only as they elucidate general questions. General theories are valuable when they help us understand the world. These are complementary not contradictory tasks. The general alone is abstract theory; the particular alone is parochial.

As we have argued throughout this paper, there are common themes to the complex study of contemporary Jewry. These could be organized into a general survey course which would outline and map the whole, fitting the particular in a more general overview. Such a course would be of value both to those in related fields of Judaica and to those in general social science disciplines interested in ethnic and religious groups.

A series of tutorials on specific topics could be organized within various social science departments to analyze in depth particular issues of concern to modern Jewish studies. These would be placed within the broader contexts of the discipline, using the methods appropriate for their study. A research seminar focused specifically on comparative Jewish contexts, drawing on faculty and students from several disciplines, would be a creative intellectual base for a doctoral program.

In an important sense, therefore, the study of contemporary Jews is no different from the study of contemporary Americans, Englishmen, Frenchmen, or whomever. The only difference is that to study Jews one must focus on cross-national analyses, since large Jewish subcommunities are located in many countries. Since Jews have occupied various social classes, political statuses, and residential niches, the comparative contexts vary in other respects as well. Explicit comparative studies—Jews cross-nationally and Jews compared with non-Jews within countries as well as cross-nationally—are required in a doctoral program.

It follows that a doctoral program in contemporary Jewish studies would require faculty in each of the departments of social science who are engaged in research on contemporary Jewries. A student entering such a doctoral program would be entering one of the fields of social science and mastering all the elements of the field. Modern Jewish studies would represent the student's specialization.

The challenge of studying modern Jewries and their communities from the perspectives of Jewish studies and the social sciences is exciting. No such comprehensive program exists in an American university. There are no major obstacles to the development of such a program, and there is every reason to consider it seriously and feel assured of its success.

Notes

1 These themes and their broader application to Jewish society and politics in the past century have been developed in Calvin Goldscheider and Alan S. Zuckerman, *The Transformation of the Jews* (University of Chicago Press, 1984).
2 See Seymour Martin Lipset, *Revolution and Counterrevolution*, (Anchor Books, 1970); and Lawrence Shofer, "The History of European Jewry: Search for a Method," in *Leo Baeck Institute Yearbook* 19 (1979): 17–36.
3 See discussions in Eric Leifer, "Competing Models of Political Mobilization: The Role of Ethnic Ties," *American Journal of Sociology* 87 (July 1981): 23–47; François Nielson, "The Flemish Movement in Belgium after World War II: A Dynamic Analysis," *American Sociological Review* 45 (February 1980): 76–94; Nathan Glazer and Daniel Patrick Moynihan, eds., *Ethnicity: Theory and Experience* (Harvard University Press, 1975).
4 See some of the essays in Glazer and Moynihan, eds., *Ethnicity*.
5 Michael Hechter, *Internal Colonialism: The Celtic Fringe in British National Development, 1536–1966* (University of California Press, 1975); J. Stone, ed., *Internal Colonialism*, special issue of *Ethnic and Racial Studies*, 2, 3 (July 1979).
6 Hechter, *Internal Colonialism*, p. 30.
7 Ibid., p. 31.
8 Ibid.; Neil Smelser, "Mechanics of Change and Adjustment to Change," in *Comparative Perspectives on Industrial Society*, ed. W. Faunce and W. Form (Little, Brown, 1969).
9 Nielson, "The Flemish Movement"; Leifer, "Competing Models"; Frederick Barth, ed., *Ethnic Groups and Boundaries: The Social Organization of Cultural Difference* (Little, Brown, 1969).
10 Alan S. Zuckerman, "New Approaches to Political Cleavage: A Theoretical Introduction," *Comparative Political Studies* (July 1982): 131–44.
11 W. Yancey et al., "Emergent Ethnicity: A Review and Reformulation,"

American Sociological Review 41 (1976): 391–402; Glazer and Moynihan, eds., *Ethnicity*

12 Edna Bonacich, "A Theory of Middlemen Minorities," *American Sociological Review* 38 (October 1973): 583–94.

13 Jacob Neusner, *The Academic Study of Judaism: Essays and Reflections*, Three Contexts of Jewish Learning, 3d Series (New York: KTAV, 1980).

14 Marshall Sklare, "Contemporary Jewish Studies," in *The Teaching of Judaics in American Universities*, ed. Leon Jick (KTAV, 1970), pp. 68–69.

References

Barth, Frederik (ed.), *Ethnic Groups and Boundaries: The Social Organization of Cultural Difference*, Little, Brown, 1969.

Bonacich, Edna, "A Theory of Middlemen Minorities," *American Sociological Review* 38 (Oct. 1973), pp. 583–94.

Glazer, Nathan and Daniel P. Moynihan (eds.), *Ethnicity: Theory and Experience*, Harvard University Press, 1975.

Goldscheider, Calvin and Alan S. Zuckerman, *The Transformation of the Jews*, University of Chicago Press, 1984.

Hechter, Michael, *Internal Colonialism: The Celtic Fringe in British National Development 1536–1966*, University of California Press, 1975.

Leifer, Eric, "Competing Models of Political Mobilization: The Role of Ethnic Ties," *American Journal of Sociology* 87 (July 1981), pp. 23–47.

Lipset, Seymour M., *Revolution and Counterrevolution*, Anchor Books, 1970.

Neusner, Jacob, *The Academic Study of Judaism: Essays and Reflections*, NY: KTAV, 1980 (Third Series: Three Contexts of Jewish Learning.)

Nielson, François, "The Flemish Movement in Belgium after World War II: A Dynamic Analysis," *American Sociological Review* 45 (Feb. 1980), pp. 76–94.

Shofer, Lawrence, "The History of European Jewry: Search for a Method," in *Leo Baeck Institute Yearbook*, 19 (1979), pp. 17–36.

Sklare, Marshall, "Contemporary Jewish Studies," in Leon Jick (ed.) *The Teaching of Judaica in American Universities*, KTAV Publishing House, Inc., 1970.

Smelser, Neil, "Mechanism of Change and Adjustment to Change," in W. Faunce and W. Form (eds.), *Comparative Perspectives on Industrial Society*, Little, Brown, 1969.

Stone, J. (ed.), *Internal Colonialism*, special issue of *Ethnic and Racial Studies* 2, 3, July, 1979.

Yancey, W., et. al., "Emergent Ethnicity: A Review and Reformulation," *American Sociological Review* 41 (1976), pp. 391–402.

Zuckerman, Alan S., "New Approaches to Political Cleavage: A Theoretical Introduction," *Comparative Political Studies* (July 1982), pp. 131–44.

5. Graduate Training in Hebrew Literature

Robert Alter

It is obvious enough that Jewish studies do not in themselves constitute a discipline but are rather a loose and perhaps uneasy alliance of disparate disciplines, involving different tools of analysis, varying languages, and far-flung geographical regions and historical eras. All this makes for special difficulties in the training of graduate students. As in any other area of academic inquiry, those of us working with doctoral students feel a primary responsibility to give them a professional competence in what we like to imagine as the most rigorous and up-to-date methods of scholarly investigation. The prospective Jewish historian should be made to grapple with all the complexities and ambiguities of gathering and sifting historical evidence; the prospective Jewish philologist should be aware of the full range of problems, diachronic and synchronic, of linguistic analysis. For someone working, say, in American history or Romance philology, the acquisition of this sort of command of a specific body of knowledge and a specific set of analytic procedures would be enough, but that is not altogether the case for the sundry fields grouped under the rubric Jewish studies. That sprawling entity, however amorphous, has certain strong lines of internal cohesion because its object is, after all, the historical experience and cultural productivity of a people that has insisted on seeing its identity as a continuous one and that has exhibited the most remarkable tenacity in holding onto key elements of its early literary and intellectual activity even as layer after layer of new texts, ideas, and outlooks were accumulated. This untiring inventiveness of the Jewish people in embedding its past in its present, even as it underwent the most radical changes through three millennia, poses a special challenge to any student in the various fields of Jewish studies. It is, of course, conceivable that a student of modern European Jewish history might complete his training without ever having studied a page of Talmud, without ever having read the medieval Jewish philosophers and poets, but he would do so at the grave risk of missing an important dimension of background in his subject which might explain many of its nuances and in some cases even its impelling forces.

The problem I have sketched out is in one respect much more acute for the study of modern Hebrew literature than for any of the other disciplines associated with Jewish studies. Let me propose a general rule-of-thumb: all literary expression, including the most avant-garde (sometimes, in fact, especially the most avant-garde), is intrinsically conservative. That is, literature is a historically evolving system in which the earlier stages are almost never discarded, in which there is a continual reusing of the earlier stages, or, from another viewpoint, a continual dialectical interplay with them. The "Oxen of the Sun" section in Joyce's *Ulysses,* in which the language progressively recapitulates the phases of English style from medieval Latin and Anglo-Saxon to late Victorian, is merely an extreme instance that exposes an underlying tendency of literary expression in general.

It would not, for example, occur to anyone to perform so unnatural an act as the writing of a poem if he had not read other poems—in most instances, many other poems and usually not just from the poet's own period. Even the most intensely personal poem, in other words, is a highly artificial form of expression dictated—or at the very least, mediated—by an elaborate set of antecedent codes and models. A twentieth-century Hebrew poet may have Mayakovsky or Rilke or Dylan Thomas in mind when he turns a particular image or attacks a particular subject, but because he writes in Hebrew, sensitive to what can be done with the indigenous resources of the language, he is often likely to shape his poem with an awareness of some or many earlier Hebrew poems, by Halevi or Hanagid, by some anonymous *payytan,* by Isaiah the son of Amotz, or whoever the case may be. As I said, this recapitulative impulse is characteristic of all literary expression, but the student of modern Hebrew literature is confronted with the sheer quantitative difficulty of working with one of the world's longest continuous literary traditions—and a tradition, to boot, in which recapitulation is intensified because of the peculiarly text-centered character of the culture. The student of Sumerian has no body of modern or medieval or Hellenistic literature to worry about; the student of French literature has a mere millennium's worth of major texts to master; the student of modern Hebrew literature has to acquire some professional literacy for three thousand years of literary productivity, from *Shirat Devorah,* the Song of Deborah, to the short stories of Devorah Baron, and beyond.

And in comparison with people in other areas of Jewish studies, the student of modern Hebrew literature finds himself perched on the top of *tel,* responsible at least in some degree for all the strata below, where others may be comfortably digging into some earlier stratum blissfully oblivious to what was accreted later. A Bible scholar's knowledge of Hebrew literature could easily stop with the Dead Sea Scrolls, though of course in a Jewish Bible scholar one would like to see some mastery of the subsequent corpus of traditional exegesis. And while I would love to have every rabbinics scholar know the free-verse poetry of Amir Gilboa or the novels of Y. H. Brenner, I must admit that no argument could be made for the relevance of such modern texts to the scholarly investigation of the rabbinic period. In contrast, the specialist in modern Hebrew literature must have some familiarity with all that has preceded in order to make real sense of his own texts.

The student of Hebrew literature, then, has to acquire competence along two different axes: a "vertical" axis, which goes back through three millennia of Hebrew expression, and which, because of the subtly and intensely recapitulative dynamic of literary discourse, can scarcely be slighted; and a "horizontal" axis, which runs through the sundry methods of analysis and theoretical considerations that constitute literary studies as a formal discipline. There are some, to be sure, who might question whether there is such a thing as a coherent discipline of literary studies—called more pointedly in Hebrew, by the Tel Aviv school, with a certain polemic thrust inspired by German usage, *mada hasifrut,* the science of literature. I shall argue that, despite the lack of consensus, and even despite the recent vehement attacks on the stability of literary interpretation from within the field itself, there is such a thing as a discipline of literary studies, with a body of concepts and methods that the student of Hebrew literature must be able to use.

Having delineated the broad contours of the problem, let me now speak more concretely about what I have learned from my experience in working with graduate students in Hebrew literature at Berkeley. This will involve some account of the distinctive features of the Berkeley program, but that, too, I would hope, may touch on certain general principles.

When I first came to Berkeley in 1967, after five years in the department of English at Columbia, I must confess that I had had no experience with coherent programs in Hebrew literature either in America or in Israel, and the only possible model in this country for such a program was the one Arnold Band had created during the several preceding years at UCLA. My appointment at Berkeley was a joint one in Hebrew and comparative literature, and the elaborately defined program for graduate students in comparative literature gave Hebrew a ready-made framework in which to spell out the details of its own requirements. As things have turned out, most of my graduate students in Hebrew literature over the years have been people doing doctorates in comparative literature with modern Hebrew as a major, rather than exclusive students of Hebrew literature working in our department of Near Eastern studies. It was fortunate for the training of students of Hebrew literature that the department of comparative literature at Berkeley happened to have the most aggressively traditionalist program in comparative literature in the country. At a time when departments of literature at other American universities were abandoning literary history as an antiquated concept in favor of more free-wheeling and theoretical approaches to the corpus of literary texts (a tendency that since has become much more pronounced), comparative literature at Berkeley was founded on the belief in the importance of literary history and of following the gradual evolution of particular literary traditions.

In practical terms, this meant that our doctoral students were obliged to master an imposing reading list (recently, this has been replaced by a sequence of required courses) that covered their major literature from its earliest extant texts to the contemporary period. There has been a pragmatic as well as an intrinsic justification for this exacting requirement. Ph.D.'s in comparative literature generally have to look for a first job in a department representing their major literature, and we wanted to be able to ensure that our students would know their major literature at least as thoroughly as someone doing a degree in that literature alone. In fact, some colleagues from neighboring departments scoffed at our historical requirements as blind devotion to pointless principle; and during a period, for example, when graduate programs in English were throwing out Anglo-Saxon and even Middle English requirements, one could make a plausible case that for the student of modern English literature, almost everything before the Renaissance was largely irrelevant and that time could more usefully be spent on other matters. I remain a little skeptical about the persuasiveness of such arguments for dispensing with the full historical range of literary tradition in the case of the modern European literatures, but in the particular case of modern Hebrew, I am entirely convinced that it is foolish even to contemplate a proposition of this sort. To respond intelligently, for example, to the poems of Avraham Ben Yitzhak Sonne without a close textual familiarity with the Book of Psalms is like trying to make sense of Thomas Mann's *Doktor Faustus* in total ignorance of the Faust story in any of its versions. To read S. Y. Agnon without having studied Mishnah and Midrash not only leaves many allusions and even some technical peculiarities of narrative presentation an enigma but makes a good deal of the language—idioms, syntax, morphology, lexical nuances—unintelligible.

Students of Hebrew literature at Berkeley, then, are obliged to prepare for their M.A. examination a chronological list of texts (at this stage, necessarily, a highly selective list) beginning with Genesis and running through the rabbinic and medieval period to the Haskalah and the later nineteenth and twentieth centuries. Before taking their doctoral examination, which is now concentrated in a period of specialization, they must have completed a sequence of fifteen courses, based on the quarter system (some may have been done before coming to Berkeley), distributed through the major historical phases and modes of expression of Hebrew literature: three courses in Bible, one in Talmud, one in Midrash, one in medieval exegesis, two in medieval poetry, and so forth. Obviously, such a set of requirements could not give anyone a professional command of three thousand years of literature, but it does ensure as nearly as formal requirements can a certain minimal literacy in the various phases of Hebrew literature.

By way of transition from my account of the vertical axis of training in Hebrew literature to the horizontal one, I should like to observe that the stress on Hebrew literary tradition, which is indispensable simply to make sense of the background of allusion and the language of many modern texts, also serves a rather different purpose. The student of Hebrew literature, precisely because of the immense stretch of time and the bewildering variety of styles and literary modes with which he is confronted, has a rare opportunity to scrutinize firsthand—which means, before all else, studying texts in their original language—a very broad variety of possibilities of literary expression. There is as much to be learned, in other words, from instructive differences as from interconnections between modern Hebrew literature and its various antecedents. With all the "influence" of earlier Hebrew literature on modern texts, I think one must concede that for the overwhelming majority of modern Hebrew poets, basic notions about poetic structure, prosody, imagery, lyric voice, and so forth are drawn from modern Western models, just as for most writers of prose fiction in Hebrew assumptions about the handling of narrative point of view, the presentation of character, the use of dialogue, description, and so forth are taken from the recent European tradition of the novel, not from the Bible or the Midrash or the medieval *maqamah*. What I am suggesting is that to understand minutely the very divergent ways in which writers over the centuries have worked with these fundamental aspects of literary expression will give the student a finer, more complicated perception of what is going on in the modern texts on which he usually concentrates because he will have a broader overview of the spectrum of possibilities of literary expression. No doubt, we would all have a subtler understanding of modern English poetry if we had a serious acquaintance with Chinese or Japanese verse, but since that is a linguistic state of bliss to which very few of us can aspire, we have a certain advantage, as students of Hebrew, in being able to read texts as disparate as those of the Italian Hebrew sonneteers, the Hebrew poets of medieval Spain, the early *payytanim*, the Job poet.

Let me offer two examples of this instructive function of the long Hebrew tradition for students of literature. A few years ago, I had the good luck to get as a new graduate student in Hebrew and comparative literature an extraordinarily gifted young woman from Israel who had done her undergraduate degree in the theoretically oriented, avowedly nonhistorical department of poetics and comparative literature at Tel Aviv University. She groaned when she learned that she would have to take a course in medieval Hebrew poetry before her M.A., her only previous experience with that body of texts having been the necessity to "go over" some of them for her high school baccalaureate exams—which was perhaps worse than not having read them at all. Since no regular course in medieval poetry was offered that year, we agreed that I would give her a tutorial in the subject. I assigned her a group of poems by Yehudah Halevi in Schirmann's annotated anthology. A week later, she came back to my office in a state of high excitement: she simply had had no idea, she said, that anything this extraordinary existed in Hebrew. Since, as it turned out, her special interest in her chosen field of descriptive poetics was metaphor, it was a real revelation for her to discover in the great medieval poets such an astonishingly rich and inventive deployment of figurative language, proceeding from assumptions about the nature of figurative language and its role in poetry fundamentally at odds with modern notions and modern poetic practice. And I might add that her encounter with these texts was instructive not only for her: over the next two months, as we tried to puzzle out together in our weekly sessions the peculiar magical artistry of these poems, I learned a good deal from her critical suggestions, in part simply because she was such a good reader, but also because she was often able to make good use of her previous linguistic work on the dynamics of metaphor in explicating these spectacularly unmodern texts.

My other example of an instructive engagement with earlier Hebrew literary texts is an experience that has had larger ramifications for the critical orientation of my students and for my own work as teacher and critic. Our program, as I have explained, requires courses in Bible and stipulates certain books of the Bible for the M.A. examination and for the older version of the Ph.D. examination. Around the mid-1970s, I began to receive complaints from my students of modern Hebrew literature that the only graduate courses in Bible offered at Berkeley were exclusively devoted to a close philological and historical scrutiny of the Book of Leviticus. It was obvious that such investigations, however valuable they might be in the field of biblical studies, could be no more than marginally relevant to a student trying to come to terms with the expressionist poetry of Uri Zvi Greenberg or the mistily subjective novellas of Uri Nissan Gnessin. Stimulated by the earliest of Meir Sternberg's and Menakhem Perry's pioneering Hebrew articles on the poetics of biblical narrative, I decided to pursue a latent interest of my own while doing something for my students by devising a seminar on biblical narrative. There were ten of us, including a couple of faithful auditors, and the students were, I am happy to say, as lively and intellectually challenging a group as any teacher could desire. Somewhat surprisingly, we all rapidly developed the sense of elation of discovering virgin territory, for though endless volumes and monographs and learned articles had been devoted to all sorts of aspects of the Bible, little had been written on its literary art that was not embarrassingly rudimentary. In our class discussions, we were struggling—but not altogether fumbling, I think—to work out new categories of analysis, and the students in their seminar papers proposed fresh and generally persuasive ways of looking at texts which conventional scholarship had abundantly discussed, but never from a rigorous literary perspective.

That first seminar on biblical narrative in 1977 remains in many ways the high point of my experience as a teacher so far (though a close second would be the seminar on biblical poetry that I offered for the first time the following year). One concrete result of the course, as some of you may have surmised, was my book *The Art of Biblical Narrative,* which was published in the summer of 1981. But what I should like to stress in regard to our concern with graduate training is the bearing of this sort of critical investigation of an ancient corpus on literary studies and on the study of modern Hebrew literature in particular. Because of Hebrew writers' hyperconsciousness of their biblical antecedents—in our own generation, for obvious cultural reasons, the Bible now far surpasses all later stages of Hebrew as a background to modern writing—there is even a limited degree of technical assimilation of biblical literary procedures in modern Hebrew literature. Criticism has long recognized, for example, that deployed on both sides of the classical caesura in Bialik's hexameters one often discovers the elegantly symmetrical lineaments of the two bicola of a line of biblical parallelistic verse. I would add, moreover, that a painstaking study of biblical prosody and of what is involved in the semantic interplay between parallel members of biblical verse enables one to see more precisely what Bialik is doing and how the biblical forms are subtly or profoundly altered as they are assimilated into a European mode of poetic expression. The technical impact of the Bible on modern Hebrew prose is much more fragmentary and oblique, but one does find certain prosewriters who, beyond allusion and imaginative *midrash*, have absorbed in their own writing certain procedures of biblical narrative, like using *Leitwörter* to articulate theme or capitalizing on the ambiguities of paratactical links in a narrative text.

As to the understanding of many broader literary issues, I cannot think of a literary corpus more rewarding to study than the Bible. This is partly because of the dimension of instructive difference to which I referred earlier. If, for example, the overwhelming preponderance of modern narrative has accustomed us to a mode of fiction that works through massive specification of circumstantial detail, one can expand one's notions about the possibilities of narrative by contemplating these wonderfully laconic biblical tales, where so much is pointedly left unsaid, where great depth of characterization and thematic development is achieved virtually without circumstantial detail. There are also, of course, continuities between the example of the Bible and later literary practice. And precisely because the biblical narratives exhibit a subtle, highly developed art with relatively little textural elaboration, certain of the primary modalities of narrative are more readily available for inspection and definition in the Bible than in many other kinds of texts. As a teacher of comparative literature, I have found with increasing frequency that I can make good illustrative use of biblical analogues in trying to explain aspects of Fielding, Balzac, Joyce, and others, and my guess is that my graduate students in Hebrew have also been discovering that their engagement with the literary artistry of the Bible offers a degree of illumination for certain general issues of literary studies.

It should be apparent that so far I have invoked rather than explained the term "literary studies." What is implied by this "horizontal axis" of the student's preparation, and what precisely is its relevance for the prospective specialist in Hebrew literature? Let me first observe that, until the creation in the late sixties of the journal *Ha-Sifrut*, which has been more concerned with general poetics and literary theory than with Hebrew literature as such, there was something peculiarly insular about the professional study of Hebrew literature, and we are not yet free of that legacy of insularity. I do not mean to suggest, of course, that the leading scholarly expositors of Hebrew literature in the past couple of generations had not read widely in European literature, but the typical relation to other literatures and, especially, to the critical study of literature was that of the autodidact (I have in mind such varying figures as Klausner, Lahover, Sadan, Kurzweil, and, still more recently, Eli Schweid). The most general consequence was an approach to Hebrew literature that was characteristically and lamentably "internal." To begin with, this sometimes led to a serious slighting of the comparative contexts of Hebrew literature. Thus, Bialik's stance as poet-prophet was constantly discussed as a simple—or, in another rhetorical vein, miraculous—continuity between the ancient Hebrew prophets and the modern poet. No notice was taken of the fact that the poet as prophet was a standard *topos* of the nineteenth-century Russian tradition which had given Bialik his most immediate models for what poetry should be, that Pushkin, for example, had written a famous poem about the poet's calling to his task based on Isaiah 6, or that such models might throw real light on poems by Bialik like *Davar* ("Mission") and *Ḥozeh Leikh Beraḥ Lekha* ("Seer, Flee Thou").

The more serious deficiency, however, of this body of criticism was that it had such shaky notions, or in some cases, no notion at all, about how to discuss the complex formal mechanisms through which literature elaborates or intimates its meanings. Literary texts were often seen in terms of the role they played in the evolution of or toward Zionism (Klausner and many others), or as expressions of the underlying spiritual problematic of modern Jewish existence (Kurzweil). Alleged influences from one Hebrew writer or school of writers to another were tirelessly catalogued, with little awareness of the ambiguities and methodological quandaries involved in any effort to describe literary influence. A good deal of this enterprise was given to impressionistic, often "lyric" evocation of the works, on the one hand, and to thematic paraphrase, on the other.

One striking symptom of the lack of a critical methodology has been the marked tendency, by no means yet abated, to subject the later works of S. Y. Agnon to allegorizing interpretation. The most egregious instance is Meshullam Tochner, who turned everything into allegory, but one finds the tendency even in a critic as shrewd as Dov Sadan, who in an unfortunately influential article transformed the haunting erotic novella *Shevuat Emunim* ("Betrothed") into a tale of Israel, the Shekhinah, and the seductive dangers of assimilation. I think it can be demonstrated that the mature Agnon of the 1940s and 1950s set a series of elaborate traps in his fiction to catch readers and especially critics prone to allegorical exegesis, while the stories and novels themselves are devised to mock and subvert allegory, proposing instead a far more ambiguous order of signification. My point is that if these critics had had a disciplined sense of how narrative texts generate meanings; of what are the relations between individual character and theme in fiction; of how modulations of point of view help define fictional statement; of what sorts of links exist in fiction between different kinds of narrators and the implied author, they would not have come to these ingenious but amateurish readings. I don't mean to suggest that there can ever be unanimity in interpretation or that there is a single "scientific" method that gives one the perfect key to a literary work, but I do believe that scrupulous attention to the formal mechanisms and generic contexts of literature at least makes it possible to exclude certain kinds of readings.

The surprising persistence of "internal" approaches to Hebrew literature was brought home to me a few years ago when another Israeli student came to Berkeley to do a doctorate, in this case someone whose training (if that is the right word here) had been entirely in Hebrew literature. Because this student arrived with an M.A., having done extensive classroom work in his major field, and because I was on leave the year after his arrival, he managed to take his doctoral examinations without having been in any of my seminars and, indeed, with a bare minimum of coursework in our program. His dissertation topic, which was wholly his choice, involved some intriguing issues of style, influence, and fictional form, but when he began delivering chapters, I discovered to my dismay that he was doing little more than writing detailed synopses of the works under discussion—supplemented, as the thesis progressed, by what amounted to Zionist homilies (for the subject of the dissertation was an avowedly Zionist writer). The two of us spent more than a year struggling over these ideological synopses that refused to become literary analyses. Improvements were introduced, enough to make the dissertation minimally acceptable. It should be obvious, however, that the writing of a dissertation can ideally complete a student's graduate training but can hardly initiate a process of education that should have been going on at least for the preceding three or four years.

Could such a student have been helped by a broad and systematic exposure to the discipline of literary studies? What concerns me, of course, is not the educability of a particular individual but whether the academic study of literature really offers a body of cumulative knowledge. Especially at this moment, when there are such widely and wildly divergent critical and theoretical approaches in vogue, in the extreme instances leaping free of the literary text to the metaphysical heavens above and the metapsychological abysses below, I suppose we should all bear in mind Samuel Johnson's gloomily brilliant words of warning in the "Preface to Shakespeare" on the changing fashions of intellectual history:

> The opinions prevalent in one age, as truths above the reach of controversy, are confuted and rejected in another, and rise again to reception in remoter times. . . . The tide of seeming knowledge which is poured over one generation, retires and leaves another naked and barren; the sudden meteors of intelligence which for a while appear to shoot their beams into the regions of obscurity, on a sudden withdraw their lustre, and leave mortals again to grope their way.

In the end, of course, in any intellectual discipline, we are all condemned to grope our way, but I would dissent from Dr. Johnson's powerfully imagined pessimism sufficiently to propose that there are often after-glimmerings of those vanished meteors which can still guide us, that we devise our own lights by an inherited luminescence, and that if we are very lucky, we may have more than an empty bushel to show to those who come after us.

Thus, the New Criticism that dominated American approaches to poetry from the 1930s through the early 1950s has long been out of fashion, and it is easy enough now to dismiss its lack of historical sense, its linguistic and epistemological naiveté, the excesses of its emphasis on irony and paradox. Nevertheless, I would argue that many of us have learned—and continue to apply—a minutely discriminating attentiveness to poetic texts, an awareness of the differential qualities of poetic language, that were not generally available before the advent of the New Criticism; and even in 1982, I feel no embarrassment in sending students of Hebrew who are floundering with poetry to read Cleanth Brooks's *The Well Wrought Urn* or Reuben Brower's *The Fields of Light*. Or again, Erich Auerbach's great study *Mimesis: The Representation of Reality in Western Literature* (1946) has been subject in the past couple of decades to stringent critique for the philosophical simplifications of its concept of representation, for the one-sidedness of its commitment to an evolution of realism in literature, for the inadequacies in its treatment of specific texts. Despite this tide of objections, and despite radical changes in intellectual fashions, *Mimesis* remains a bench mark in literary studies. It is hard, for example, to discuss the emergence of the realistic novel without somehow confronting Auerbach's seminal readings of Prévost, Stendhal, Balzac, and Zola; and even his method of analysis, which moves from a consideration of characteristic grammar, syntax, diction, imagery, and the like, to generalizations about mimetic assumptions, is still, with modifications, eminently usable.

Let me offer one more specific example of cumulative knowledge in literary studies from the area of prose fiction, where a good deal of my teaching and critical work have been concentrated. Ever since Henry James's prefaces to the New York Edition of his novels at the beginning of the century, there has been considerable awareness in the English-speaking world of the strategic importance of narrative point of view in the novel. James's outlook was codified in a rather programmatic way by Percy Lubbock in *The Craft of Fiction* (1923), and the distinctions Lubbock laid down continued to have quasi-legislative authority in many circles for the next four decades. Some twenty years ago, Wayne Booth's *The Rhetoric of Fiction* provided a major corrective to Lubbock and James by defending the artistic virtues of narratorial "telling" (that is, explicit statement and commentary) over against "showing" (that is, the seemingly immediate and dramatic rendering of narrative event from a character's point of view). Booth also introduced useful demarcations between narrator and implied author, reliable narrator and various kinds of unreliable narrator. The French narratologists of the later sixties and early seventies provided a very different conceptual framework for considering these issues, Gérard Genette being the most distinguished of these analysts. In 1978, Dorrit Cohn published *Transparent Minds*, a lucid study of the modes of representation of consciousness in fiction, which built on both the Anglo-American and the Continental critical traditions and proposed sharper, more sensible terms and distinctions than had any of her predecessors.

When I teach, for example, a seminar on the development of the Hebrew novella, I find it pedagogically indispensable to make students aware of this body of criticism and the concepts it proposes for general use. Even supposedly up-to-date Hebrew studies of a writer like Gnessin speak loosely about "interior monologue" or "stream of consciousness" in his fiction (another reflection of the legacy of insularity), and I try to get students to make more precise discriminations than that about narrative technique. It is hard to see what is happening in the Hebrew novella from Gnessin to Agnon to David Fogel without minute critical perception of the modulations in narrative point of view, and so I discover that a course on this Hebrew topic necessarily involves considerations of the "poetics of prose" and, at least methodologically, does not differ much from teaching Flaubert or Nabokov or Virginia Woolf.

In any process of advanced education, no teacher should take too much credit for himself because it is obviously the student who has to do a large part of his own educating. I would like to conclude with an example of such self-education which seems to me an instructive success story, particularly in regard to the understanding of the horizontal axis of Hebrew literary training. About three years ago, one of my American students of Hebrew and comparative literature began work on a dissertation involving, at least initially, images of the hero in three generations of Hebrew novelists. On the face of it, this was the sort of topic that might have easily lent itself to the thematic paraphrase of which past Hebrew criticism has been so often enamored. What the student discovered as he wrestled with the topic was that he could not really discuss the treatment of the protagonist in his chosen novels without confronting certain underlying issues of what is involved in fictional characterization. This led him to the French structuralist tradition, to the Russian Formalists behind so much of recent French thinking about literature, and to a consideration of what was lacking in these approaches as well as what might be learned from them—for, in fact, the phenomenon of fictional character has not proved as amenable to formal analysis as other aspects of narrative, and much remains to be done on the theory of character.

The result of this dissertation writer's inquiries was a set of carefully considered, formally precise discriminations about his three novelists that went beyond the commonplaces of Hebrew literary history and that, in the case of one of the writers discussed, proposed a new and plausible solution to what had long been a crux of critical debate on the role of the narrator in that novelist's fictional world.

There may be, finally, a certain intrinsic advantage in the location of the various fields of Jewish studies within the setting of the American university. In Israel, where there are sizable departments of Hebrew literature, rabbinics, Bible, Jewish history, and so forth, Jewish studies, with such institutional resources and numbers, may have the luxury of being relatively closed off from what is going on in the surrounding disciplines. In an American university, on the other hand, any one of the fields just mentioned is bound to be an exotic plant and a tiny academic minority, and so there is a natural gravitation, with or without departmental links, toward the larger disciplinary sphere within the university that is most relevant to the area of Judaica in question. At least in my own field, I find this a fortunate circumstance, and I suspect that is true as well in the other fields of Jewish studies.

Students and teachers alike, we are obliged to live at the intersection of axes running along the discipline, with all the intricacies of its sundry methodologies, and down into the Jewish past, with all the rich and bewildering variegation of its accumulated layers. As I have been arguing, these double claims are particularly urgent on the student of modern Hebrew literature. You can't read Mendele, you can't make sense of his language or the inventive play of his allusions, without knowing Bible and Talmud and liturgy and Midrash—and without some awareness of the Yiddish in which his major achievements were first cast. But because Mendele's work is not only Hebrew but also artful fiction, you can't read him, you can't make sense of his artifices of narration and his fictional structures, without knowing a good deal about the dynamics of narrative. To respond fully to both sets of claims in a scant four or five years of graduate education is of course an impossible task but I suspect that the best of our graduate students, properly encouraged, will show the resourcefulness and dedication to approximate the impossible where it cannot be fully achieved.

6. Graduate Education in Modern Hebrew Literature

Arnold J. Band

Conventional academic writing normally shuns the projection of the subject into the discourse: we write in the third person, often in the mysterious passive, at times in the self-effacing "we" which is supposed to connote decorum. I find myself constrained, particularly in this paper, to indulge in the promiscuous "I" not only to avoid an intimation of false modesty, but also to set the proper perspective for my remarks which, by the very nature of the topic, have to be experiential. And since it is my experience I have to discuss, I see no purpose in tranparent masquerade. The experience I refer to is not only my own work as a director of graduate studies confronted with the daily problems of guiding doctoral candidates, but the concomitance of my teaching career with a phenomenon in the history of Judaics scholarship which I have called elsewhere "the academization of modern Hebrew literature." The concomitance, of course, was fortuitous, but without some description of what others have done, I cannot present what motivated my choices.

By "academization" we mean not only the entrenchment of the area study in the academy, but—of greater import—the adoption and application of academic norms of research, however varied and controversial they might be. In this respect, modern Hebrew literature has differed radically from the more established fields of Jewish studies: while biblical or medieval scholarship could rely, in the late 1940s, upon at least a century of professional scholarship, modern Hebrew literature wallowed in dilettantism and its normal genre of expression was the impressionistic essay. The first generation of somewhat orderly scholars had just died or retired; Shapira was killed in the Kovna ghetto in 1943; Lahover died in Tel Aviv in 1947;

and Klausner retired from his post at the Hebrew University in 1948. They did not leave behind them either viable methods or useful scholarly tools, or a definable group of successors.

The state of the art at that period was indeed primitive, to say the least. Our basic text was Lahover's *Toldot HaSifrut Ha'ivrit Hahadashah*, which stops in the first decade of this century and was an uneasy compromise between a high school textbook and an attempt at historical summation. Klausner's *Historia Shel HaSifrut Ha'ivrit Hahadashah* was completed only in 1950 and reaches Mendele; the limitations of Klausner's work, for all its usefulness as a fairly reliable source of information, are well known and need no elaboration here. For all practical purposes, Hebrew literature did not exist as an area of academic research and instruction in 1948, the year the State of Israel was created and Yosef Klausner retired from his chair at the Hebrew University, the only chair at that time in this area in the entire world. While one might argue that modern literature was added to academic curricula throughout the Western world only in the 1930s, one must grant that the great universities which hesitated to introduce modern literature taught premodern literature well and had done so for some time. We had no such tradition in the area of Jewish studies. Klausner himself, it must be said, scrupulously distinguished between what he considered the object of legitimate scholarship, i.e., Hebrew literature before his time, and what was the object of his descriptive, impressionistic essays, i.e., anything after Mendele.

A significant change can be detected in the early 1950s in Israel centered on three figures: Halkin, Sadan, and Kurzweil, all, ironically, decidedly nonacademic—or even antiacademic—personalities who made their way into academic circles. Though a systematic, rationalized study of modern Hebrew literature was not to be found even in Jerusalem, one did get the feeling that new currents were sweeping through the pages of literary journals. Halkin himself introduced some of the ideas of the New Criticism which had taken root in America in the 1940s. Baruch Kurzweil, aping Karl Krauss, relentlessly attacked the presuppositions of much of Zionist literary criticism and revealed in many literary works, primarily those of Agnon and Greenberg, patterns of motifs which had escaped previous readers. Dov Sadan applied his phenomenal knowledge of Hebrew, Yiddish, and German literatures to countless studies of literary problems in a method so marvelously protean as to be untransmissible. While the floodgates of critical interest were opened wide in the early 1950s, no effort was made to channel the new ideas, to systematize the instruction of literature on an advanced level, to guide and conduct orderly literary study projects. It is no accident that none of these three seminal figures—Halkin, Kurzweil, or Sadan—has produced a sustained, focused literary study which transcends the scope of the essay.

The bottom line of the ledger we have recorded above should be very clear: if modern Hebrew literature was what attracted you in the 1950s, you had in your field no teachers or models of the stature of Fritz Baer, or Gershom Scholem, or Salo Baron, or Harry Wolfson. And you had for your study no periodicals of the quality of *Tarbiz* or *Zion* or the *JQR* (in its better days) or HUCA. You did have *Moznayim* and *HaDoar*.

If we take the bottom line mentioned above as our base line, we can arrive at a description of the state of the art today which will have the proper historical perspective. Let us begin with an obvious institutional fact: modern Hebrew literature is taught today in a wide variety of academic institutions. If we were to cite only those institutions which offer a doctoral program, we would have to mention the Hebrew University, Tel Aviv University, and Bar-Ilan in Israel; Columbia, Brandeis, and the Jewish Theological Seminary on the East Coast; UCLA and Berkeley on the West Coast. Haifa and Beer Sheva have departments of Hebrew literature, and individual instructors hold posts in this country in at least a dozen universities and at all the Hebrew colleges and seminaries. The study of modern Hebrew literature has found its place in the academy as have many other areas of Jewish studies over the past twenty years. While one would expect the inclusion of the more traditional areas of Jewish studies in the curriculum since they are purely academic topics and have had a distinguished history of scholarship between 1955, one is pleasantly surprised to find Hebrew literature so widely represented. That field had no tradition of scholarship. There is no doubt in my mind that the emergence of Israel as a viable state with a distinctive culture has made this area of Jewish studies acceptable.

And yet, when we turn to the qualitative aspect of academization, the introduction of more rigorous norms of scholarship and the development of criteria and techniques for the training of graduate students, we find relatively little evidence of progress until the middle

1960s. The three major professors of modern Hebrew literature (Halkin, Sadan, and Kurzweil) were nearing retirement, and their disciples had either left for other fields or not yet earned the standard academic recognition: the granting of the Ph.D. or the publication of a significant scholarly monograph. More often than not, these disciples had to fend for themselves, often at great distances from their home univerities since they could not learn methods of literary scholarship from other literary departments in Israeli universities which are singularly weak in the humanities (with the obvious exception of Judaics) even today. If we take as our model the English departments of reputable universities in the United States or England, the failings of the Israeli institutions before the middle 1960s becomes evident. The situation in that period was even worse outside Israel.

By the mid-1960s, one begins to notice the signs of a new intellectual climate: articles exhibiting a consciousness of either academic rigor or contemporary international schools of criticism usually situated in academic environments begin to appear in greater numbers. The students of the fifties—Shaked, Miron, and Hrushovski, in particular—are the names one encounters most frequently in articles and conversations. And though it is difficult to point to any specific filiation, one can detect in their writing both echoes of their teachers or dialectic departures from their methods—or lack thereof. Unlike their contemporaries in the more traditional areas of Jewish studies, they did not follow the conservative root of philological positivism, but struck out in a variety of directions, mostly formalistic and ahistorical: American, Russian, German, and French. In turn, these scholars, recently tenured at their various universities, began to influence their own students so that by the late sixties one senses a veritable surge toward a more academic type of criticism powerful enough to alarm the more impressionistic and conservative critics of *Agudat HaSoferim* and the popular weekly literary supplements— even though many of the new academic critics also wrote and continue to write popular literary essays.

When I began to set up shop at UCLA and found myself confronted with several serious graduate students in the second year of my career there, I had to refine some of the notions which I had already formulated. I knew, for instance, that I had no visible models to copy

Graduate Education in Modern Hebrew Literature 99

within my own discipline: I was not interested in continuing Klausnerian positivism or offering the ideologically oriented essay as the criterion of serious literary study. I admired, even envied, the erudition and discipline of a variety of Judaic scholars, but since their interest were essentially philological and shied away from what I considered literary questions, there was not much to be learned there beyond rigor and scholarly integrity. My graduate training in comparative literature provided both the scope of reading and the mode of thinking of a literary scholar, but no rationalized progression of study or understanding of the specific problems of modern Hebrew literature. We should not forget, furthermore, that in the first decade of the existence of the State of Israel, modern Hebrew literature was a totally unknown quantity in most American universities (not that the situation is that much better today), and Hebrew was some sort of exotic language. One fact the university did know was that Jews were a pathologically bookish people and wrote many books in many languages. I exploited this tidbit of information fully: I ordered books, serials, microfilms of periodicals, entire libraries, and even persuaded the librarians to hire a Judaica bibliographer.

Having neither a personal nor an institutional model to follow, I was free to work out my own approach. Since I began with the assumption that I was training literary scholars and not bibliographers, I dispensed with the mechanical dissemination or dictation of a bibliography of primary and secondary sources, a time-honored technique which frees the instructor from any meaningful confrontation with his students and condemns the students either to prodigious bibliographic expertise or equally prodigious intellectual chicanery. Instead, I selected, at first, a limited corpus of texts central to the emerging "Great Tradition" of modern Hebrew literature (the reference here is to F. R. Leavis who has much to teach us about the function of teaching literature in universities) and, together with my better students, formulated the proper literary questions to ask of each text. Believing, as I do, that the point of departure and the guiding principle of any literary discussion must be the "literariness of the text" (a Russian Formalist concept) much of what I began to do and still do involves the close reading of texts. The close reading, of course, is more than a necessary pedagogical device; it is the rationale, the driving principle behind all the various aspects of the graduate student's training: the skills to be acquired, the languages to be learned, the courses to be taken or created, the types of papers to be written, the reading lists to be covered, and finally the shape of the comprehensive examinations and the dissertation. And though I do not espouse Stanley Fish's position on interpretive freedom, I do think a student should understand why one might ask, "Is there a text in this class?" The student, I contend, must at all times understand exactly why a requirement is being made, how some exercise is designed to enable him/her to read a literary text more intelligently and sensitively, operations which include the historical contextualization of the literary work.

Before offering a concrete example of this fusion of problem conceptualizing with curriculum construction, I should attempt to differentiate—to some extent—between two categories, two modes of thought which we ordinarily confuse, even when such confusion is avoidable. (I will grant that at times it is unavoidable.) On the one hand there are academic disciplines such as history, philosophy, linguistics, or literature, each with its own way of looking at reality and its own set of legitimate questions. On the other hand, there are area studies taken in the broad or narrow sense. In the broadest sense they embrace entire cultures such as classics, or American studies, or Jewish studies. In the narrower sense they may be limited to a period, an institution, or a literary corpus. For example: What is the Bible or the Talmud? A discipline or an area study? These are not idle questions since they ultimately determine both the nature of our work and our construction of graduate programs.

Now, to concretize the process I have been describing I shall select as my model text the first short stanza of Bialik's "Levadi," precisely because it is so well known:

Kulom nóso horú'aḥ, kulom sóḥaf ho'ór,
Shiroh hadóshoh es bóker ḥayéhem hirnínoh;
Va'aní, gozol rákh, nishtakáhti milév
Taḥas kánfe hashkhínoh.

It should be obvious that Bialik's Hebrew is so rich from both a lexical and grammatical point of view, that the student cannot possibly read the poem—which must be read in its original language—

without a solid knowledge of Hebrew which so few of our graduate students have today. Here we confront our first major problem which does not face all graduate students in Jewish studies: while you can possibly begin graduate studies in some areas of Jewish studies with a minimum knowledge of Hebrew—let us say, two or three years of college Hebrew—you can do nothing in modern literature without considerably more than four years of undergraduate Hebrew at a good university. The lexical problem, for instance, is not merely the connotation of "noso hor'ah" but the provenance of the phrase "shiroh hadoshoh" or the multitudinous ramifications of the term "taḥas kanfe hashkhinoh." Whoever has taught this poem to a class is familiar with the problem: either there are students who can respond to the embedded terms or the time must be spent explaining connotations. For modern Hebrew literature, a substantial knowledge of Hebrew is clearly a prerequisite for graduate study, a prerequisite which becomes painfully acute when one wants to teach a three-hundred-page novel in the normal two-week period. It's not the same as doing a chapter of Bible or even a pericope of Midrash in the same period.

Once one is blessed with a student who can read this text without too much assistance, one is, theoretically, in the normal position of the director of first-year graduate studies. One plans to proceed along the two axes mentioned above: the disciplinary and the area study. One must teach the student how to read a literary text (or, more important, what a literary text is), and one must broaden his knowledge of the area. At times, however, one discovers that the type of student who might have the rich Hebraic background unconsciously resists learning how to read a literary text. The student who can recognize the provenance of "shiroh hadoshoh" or the deep emotional impact of "taḥas kanfe hashkhinoh" often comes from a *yeshiva* background where irony, metaphor, textual subversion are not the staples of pedagogical discussion—though they very well might be present in the text itself. Proof of this resistance can be found in the normative explication of this poem which still, in 1982, describes the poetic voice as simply plaintive, at most, self-pitying, when it is actually also bitterly scornful and supremely arrogant. After all, how substantial are Bialik's "kulom" if they are easily swept away by the wind (or new spirits) and sing a "shiroh hadoshoh" (which the redeemed Israelites sang at the sea) in praise of some new ideology? Or what Jew would dare claim to be on such intimate—even erotic—terms with the Shekhinah? Certainly not a despondent *yeshiva bochur!* Bialik had a very high and secure opinion of his status.

I therefore discover that precisely those students who have the richest linguistic, hence area, training are the ones who require the most extensive literary exposure, both in my seminars and in the various criticism and general literature courses offered by the university. In addition to criticism or theory of literature courses, I must persuade them to take a variety of comparative literature courses dealing primarily with the modern period.

To participate in these courses, one often needs French or German which are, in any case, required by the university. The linguistic requirements, however, do not stop here. Since so much of modern Hebrew literature is inextricably bound up with modern Yiddish literature, I insist on two examinations in Yiddish: one in the ability to read a critical article (for the M.A.) and the other designed to demonstrate the ability to analyze both Yiddish prose and poetry of the modern period. Fortunately, we have a fine Yiddish instructor to whom I can entrust these students. (Incidentally, to my knowledge, no Israeli university has this Yiddish requirement, and I think few if any American universities insist upon this requirement.) If the student happens to be registered under Near Eastern languages rather than under comparative literature—both are possible—the student must also take a term of Aramaic since all graduate students are required to take two area languages allied to their main "Near Eastern" language.

The two tracks of the doctorate, one through the department of Near Eastern languages, the other through comparative literature, are a fairly recent development—of the past five years—and each raises interesting methodological problems. The original Near Eastern track required broader area knowledge, while the newer comparative literature track stresses the disciplinary aspects. Under the Near Eastern track, the student was prepared for examinations in four areas: modern Hebrew, premodern Hebrew, Jewish history, and Yiddish literature. The comparative literature track might seem only slightly different, but the emphasis and approach turn out to shape a different focus. Again there are four areas: modern Hebrew literature, premodern Hebrew literature (though, I must admit, by no means as extensively covered as in Near Eastern languages), Yiddish literature, and another literature, German, French, Russian, or even English. Though I remain the director of doctoral studies of the students in both areas (my appointment is in both areas) there is no question that the students in the Near Eastern track receive a slightly different perspective than those in comparative literature. Those in Near Eastern will be doing course work in more traditional historical and philological modes, and their dissertations will reflect this training. Those in comparative literature will be working more in theoretical literary and comparative topics. In both cases, all work is done in Hebrew: the reading of texts, the discussion, both oral and written, the analytical term papers, etc. Since I work in both modes—the Near Eastern and the comparative literature—and believe that a thesis must be tailored to fit the personality of the student, my guidance is shaped by the orientation of the student. In other words, I do not expect the student to be a clone of me—a subliminal expectation too frequent in the academic world.

In either case, the skills demanded are formidable, and the usual course takes some seven years after the B.A. or four after the M.A., even if these degrees were granted by an Israeli institution. The Israeli student, I have discovered, usually needs at least a year to learn enough English to read a critical article properly or write a scholarly paper with some grace.

Returning to the Bialik poem, for instance, I would expect the student to know the linguistic springs of the irony (a literary and philological problem) and the writings of Bialik's predecessors and contemporaries. I would—to be more specific—demand an explanation of the impact of the use of the anapest in this poem of 1902, a truly innovative act in a generation intoxicated by the more normative amphibrach. I would expect the student to compare this poem with another poem, "'Im dimdume hahamoh," written in the same year, a comparison designed to trace linguistic parallels and mood shifts. I have my students peruse the newspapers of the weeks preceding the publication of the poem to see what the intellectual atmosphere and the mode of discourse were at that period.

The seminar courses are designed to vary from year to year, for two reasons: I feel students need maximal exposure to different types of writers and courses, and I myself am interested in different problems at different times. When I believe there should be an integral nexus between the instructor's research and the student's training, a reasonable balance must be maintained. While I could have given a new seminar on Agnon every year, thus covering a variety of problems which need treatment, I did not follow this exploitative method; had I done so, I would, of course, have doubled or trebled my publications, but would have done my students a gross injustice. As a result, I have never, in the twenty years I have been giving graduate seminars, offered the same course twice. While I have paid for this variety with somewhat diminished publication, I have learned a great deal—and have drawers full of fragmentary articles waiting to be developed—and my students have shared my adventures. These courses may be monographic, devoted to the work of one writer; generic, focusing on one genre, e.g. the novel, the lyrical poem, the Hasidic tale; or historic, dealing with a specific period or center.

At some point in the graduate career, the student should be encouraged to spend an academic year at an Israeli university, probably in Jerusalem where Judaic studies are concentrated. While not all students can manage to get away for a year or finance such a study year in Jerusalem, I find the year's study in Israel most beneficial for students in modern Hebrew literature. To begin with, our students are isolated from their natural colleagues—other graduate students in this area. In most cases, they do not get enough exposure to other scholars and mentors. And whether or not we approve of the scholarly method espoused in a certain circle of Israeli scholars, it cannot be denied that the very concentration of scholars in one place adds a dimension of breadth—albeit, sometimes only bibliographic—which is invaluable. When it comes to modern Hebrew literature, the logic for studying in Israel is no different from that for studying in Paris for the student of French literature. That is the center; that is where the living literature is published, most intensely discussed, critiqued, etc.

The university requirements of comprehensive examinations and a doctoral thesis can be rationalized to serve the educational needs of the student, if both normally mandatory goals are conceived of as progressive stages of intellectual growth. If the student has a fairly clear, acceptable thesis topic in mind before approaching the comprehensives, the reading list for the examinations (which should always be clearly delineated, even circulated to all examiners and filed) can be tailored to prepare the student to move immediately from examination preparation to advanced work on the dissertation. If the student has no clear thesis in mind, the reading list can still be designed to stress the student's natural strength—poetry, let us say, rather than prose—with the hope that from the reading certain ideas and interests will develop which might form the basis of the doctoral thesis. The actual process of the examination can be rationalized and humanized. There is no compelling educational reason for having a student sit for four examinations in two weeks; the period between examinations can be lengthened so that the learning experience will be valuable, even pleasurable. I often offer my better students the option of participating in the writing of the examination which is, in itself, part of the examination: after all, we should be teaching not only how to answer, but what to ask. The writing of the thesis, thus, is an integral climax to an educational process which has been rationalized, explained, and understood throughout. We have, incidentally, done away with the thesis defense as a relic of a Continental university system whose methods and suppositions are alien to ours.

The mode of discourse I have selected for this paper has been personal and descriptive, not only because it is my experience—however rationalized—which I am describing, but because I believe that the study of literature, particularly modern literature, is an uncommonly personal experience in the academic world. I therefore conceive of graduate teaching as a very personal experience, demanding the profound engagement of the teacher with the student's engagement with the text. Stated most simply: among other things, a student has to tell me what poem he likes and, perhaps more significantly, why he likes it—questions rarely asked in other disciplines. Such intense involvement is, to be sure, both rewarding and exhausting, often frustrating, but I cannot teach in any other way. A student who prefers the ordinary course of autodidacticism or benign neglect should go elsewhere.

7. The Role of Language in Graduate Programs of Jewish Studies

Baruch A. Levine

It is not difficult to describe in purely curricular terms what the role of language is in most graduate programs of Jewish studies at the present time. However we define the field we call Jewish studies, our graduate programs must inevitably require of the student an adequate degree of access to primary sources preserved in languages other than English or the modern European languages. This places our field in the same ballpark with Islamic, classical, Assyriological, and East Asian studies, to mention areas with similar types of language requirements.

Historically, Hebrew has been the primary language of access in Judaic learning, a role only further enhanced by the Hebraic culture of modern Israel. There are, of course, other important "Jewish languages," to use a term which figured in the title of the regional conferences held several years ago under the auspices of the Association for Jewish Studies. The presentations made at those conferences have since been edited by Herbert Paper, and published by the association. They afford an overview of the history of Jewish languages.

A Jewish language is one that has been used by a Jewish community as a spoken or written language, or both. There are languages which never became "Jewish" in this way, but which are nevertheless relevant to Jewish studies by reason of cultural and linguistic affinity. This category would apply especially to some of the ancient Semitic languages.

In most North American institutions of higher learning, the curriculum situation does, indeed, bear some resemblance to what obtains in departments of classics. One observes in both cases, and within the same recent period, a distinct trend away from language, and from study of texts in their original languages, in the direction of history and "civilization," which is a catch-all term. Literature is more often studied in translation. The old anecdote comes to mind about parsing Greek and Latin verbs as the major task of the classicist. This was one way of poking fun at the obsession with grammar.

In a similar way, programs in Jewish studies have been advocated to faculties and administrations on the very basis that they will address needs not met by earlier programs, which focused on languages and texts. Where enlightenment has prevailed, an integration of broader concepts with more traditional attitudes has been possible. In other situations, however, the two emphases—language and civilization—tend to compete with each other, and may even be perceived as antithetical to each other.

We had a recent graduate student at New York University who reflected this polarization. When he began his studies, as he saw it at the time, there were two ways to go: the narrow, technical way of language and philology, or the broad, reflective way of history, ideas, and literary themes. These were his own characterizations. I cite this case because such polarized thinking is understandable, given the current academic environment. Needless to say, I find the mere suggestion that language and ideas, or language and history, are polar alternatives to represent a basic misunderstanding of the role of language.

There will probably be greater balance in the coming years. The trend away from language has peaked. There has been significant progress in comprehending the phenomenon of language in recent decades, and it is realized that the role of language had been misunderstood. We deceive ourselves when we try to avoid the burden of a language curriculum, because language is more than a tool or skill in the service of other educational goals; it is of the nature of the materials we study. We have also had the opportunity of observing students who emerge from "language-less" graduate programs, and their limitations are patent!

Perhaps at this point I should describe the graduate program in which I have been participating for the past fourteen years. It is a limited program in Bible, rabbinics, and ancient Semitic languages operating within a department of Near Eastern languages and literature, in which Arabic and Persian are also taught, as well as history. I will outline what a graduate student undergoes in the effort to prepare for a scholarly career in Bible, Semitics, or history of early or late antiquity. These subjects are normally included in programs of Jewish studies, either integrally or on a cross-disciplinary basis.

If we assume a three-to-four-year sequence of class work, and dissertation colloquia, students in this program at New York University will study Hebrew intensively, along with Aramaic, Ugaritic, Phoenician, ancient Hebrew epigraphy, and, in most cases, Akkadian for two years. Some students include Arabic, Greek, etc. The instructional approach is primarily textual, and it is geared to relate language training to the actual materials under study.

A graduate student should be able, at the conclusion of this course of study, to do original work on biblical and other Near Eastern texts, using linguistic, exegetical, and literary methods of analysis. We encourage the study of postbiblical Hebrew, and Hebrew and Aramaic sources, even for students of Bible and the ancient Near East. Recently we have added a faculty person in medieval Hebrew literature, and our plan is to complete the language-literature picture with a faculty person in modern Hebrew literature, as well. We are also moving to include more systematic study of history, with proseminars in ancient history and the history of the subsequent periods of Jewish experience.

With respect to the Hebrew Bible, which stands at the center of the ancient studies program, the student should understand its place as an ancient Near Eastern document, as well as a monument of Jewish religious civilization, two appreciations we do not regard as contradictory. Most of all, the student should know enough, and be sufficiently independent in his capabilities, so as to utilize original source materials without relying on the interpretations of others, or on their translations and editions.

The theory underlying the program just described can best be stated in the form of a question: What do we know when we know a language; what is it that we then perceive that would be missing from our perceptions without language study?

I begin with the observation that Judaic creativity is best appreciated when we are equipped intellectually to view it within its larger universes. The historical experience of the Jewish people has been such that the primary sources which inform us of that experience often bear an intimate relation to other, more comprehensive cultures, more so than is true of societies that have stayed together throughout most of their history. One expression of this intimacy is that Judaic source materials are often preserved in the language of a larger culture. When we add to the demographic factors of Jewish experience a complex of attitudes and responses entertained by various Jewish communities throughout history toward their universes, we see that language patterns are more than technically informative.

It would be considerably speculative to venture a history of the appropriation of the Hebrew language itself as a Jewish language, but we can be quite precise about the process of Aramaization. It is one of the most pervasive and extensive cultural phenomena on record. It greatly affected the linguistic character of ancient Jewish communities.

The main fact that is often obscured in our perceptions is that Aramaic became a Jewish language because it was, or had become, the language of large and powerful societies and empires within which Jewish communities, inside and outside the land of Israel, lived and flourished. We know, thanks to the likes of Hayim Tadmor, that the process of Aramaization began to accelerate in the neo-Assyrian period, when the imperial Assyrians employed the language of Syria, their western zone, for administering the empire. By the neo-Babylonian period, toward the end of the seventh pre-Christian century, the Aramaic language of Syria had become a principal language of Mesopotamia, as well. Hezekiah's request of the Assyrian general besieging Jerusalem in the year 701 B.C.E. that he speak Aramaic, lest the people understand him in Judean Hebrew and become demoralized, would not have made much sense a century or so later, when many more Judeans would have undoubtedly known Aramaic.

In the subsequent, Achaemenid period Aramaic became the undisputed imperial language of the Persians. Once Jewish communities began to use Aramaic, the ground was laid for its absorption as a language of Bible translation, then of Talmudic discourse and prayer. To begin with, therefore, Aramaic was the language of the larger universe, or universes, in which the major Jewish communities had flourished. Once appropriation occurred, the attachment between

Jews and Aramaic was further enhanced. Aramaic affected Hebrew not only in terms of lexicon, but as regards syntax, morphology, and the Hebrew tense system. Conversely, Jews affected Aramaic, but that is getting ahead of our story.

I have taken the time to review these facts of Jewish history and ancient Near Eastern cultural development because I sense that their implications are not fully understood. After twenty years or more of studying and teaching Aramaic, and accomplishing studies of Aramaic texts, I still experience inner resistance to these facts of history myself. This may happen, for example, when I encounter a term of reference in a non-Jewish source, known to me primarily from a Jewish source. Let us suppose that I encounter a term in a Christian, Syriac chronicle, and immediately associate it with one known to me from a Talmudic, Aramaic source. (The reverse also happens, of course: I may identify a Talmudic term with a Syriac term.) In either event, I recognize that in many cases neither culture took from the other, but that both drew from the larger, Aramaic universe in which they both flourished. This is so, even though Christian literature itself often reflects a stratum of Jewish content to start with.

The point is that what I had identified uncritically as something specifically Jewish was not so at all. I can go back to the common culture, and I can sense that the two communities—the eastern Jewish and the eastern Christian—although differentiated, continued to use a diction drawn from the same general civilization.

Having said this, I should point out that there are cases where Aramaic diction originating in the Jewish communities affected Christian Syriac, and even Mandaic, because when several communities live within the same general culture they may influence one another. When, for instance, one encounters Jewish-Aramaic formulas of divorce in Syriac, even in Mandaic magical bowls, as well as in Jewish magical bowls, it is quite likely that these formulas were learned from the many Jewish magical practitioners who operated in places like Nippur during the fifth and sixth Christian centuries.

To this point, I have actually been speaking of two discrete but closely related factors: universe, and diction. These two factors reveal the subtle interplay of the synchronic and the diachronic in the relation of language to culture. Appropriation from a larger universe is synchronic, whereas diction is more a synchronic process, more of a developing phenomenon.

If I may cite an example from the biblical period which illustrates how two groups, living within the same common culture, may share common diction, I would refer to the Mesha inscription. It is written in Moabite, another of the Canaanite dialects, or languages, if you will, very similar to biblical Hebrew. This royal inscription records events of the mid-ninth century B.C.E., and refers to the Omriad dynasty of northern Israel. We read that Kemosh, the national god of the Moabites, had become enraged at his land and had handed it over to the Israelites. The Moabite verb used to connote wrath is *'anaph*, a denominative of *'anp/'app*, referring to the flaring of the nostrils, or, possibly, to facial contortion as an expression of rage. The same verb is used in the Hebrew Bible, especially in what we call Deuteronomistic literature (see Deut. 9:8, 1 Kings 8:46, 2 Kings 17:18, and Psalms 60:3, 79:5, 86:6). Furthermore, the so-called "holy war" theology is expressed quite clearly in the Moabite inscription through the verb *heherim*, "to condemn, proscribe, devote." This verb also connotes proscription in the Deuteronomistic literature of the Hebrew Bible (see Deut. 3:6, 7:2, 13:6, etc.). Like the God of Israel, Kemosh commands his chosen king to wage war, and then devote the spoils of war to him.

Since it is unlikely that the Moabite author of the ninth century learned this diction from the biblical Deuteronomist, or vice versa, I find it most reasonable to conclude that North Israelites, Judeans, and Moabites lived in the same Canaanite universe, where certain terms of reference, expressive of basic theological concepts, were current. This is what Morton Smith has called the "common theology" of the ancient Near East; in this case, somewhat more concentrated in scope.

Prior to knowing the diction of the Moabite inscription, I had considered these notions to be distinctly, if not uniquely, biblical. In fact, they are integral to the prophetic interpretation of history, on the meaning of victory and the reasons for defeat. They have to do with primary traditions on the conquest of Canaan. In other words, they strike at notions endemic to biblical historiography. And yet, there is nothing specifically monotheistic about them, or uniquely Israelite, for that matter.

Before I am criticized for being overly comparative and less than adequately contrastive, I hasten to assure you that Israelite writers did things with these notions which I doubt the Moabite writers could have done. And yet, the realization that Israelite religion and biblical historiography are built with some of the same blocks as one finds in a Moabite royal annal is both unsettling and extremely enlightening. This realization comes from perceptions of language and diction.

Max Weinreich shows us another facet of diction in his fascinating study, *A History of the Yiddish Language*. He classifies Yiddish as a fusion language, and treats it through the methodology of sociolinguistics. Through many diverse examples taken from Yiddish diction he traces what happened to Hebrew and traditional idiom, as well as what happened to German, once these components became fused in the language of a closely knit network of Jewish communities.

In Yiddish, as Weinreich analyzes its structure and development, we observe how the values and attitudes of a community determine how it expresses itself, and how modes of expression achieve a life of their own, in turn affecting attitudes and values. I'm not certain one could do the same kind of study on Aramaic as Weinreich did on Yiddish, but his exercise might provide us with some valuable methods, nevertheless. In the medieval period, certain versions of Jewish Aramaic approached the character of a fusion language. At earlier periods, Persian was transmitted extensively through the medium of Aramaic.

What do we know, then, when we know language? We learn how Jewish cultures were formed under certain historical conditions of external contact, lateral coexistence, and internal cultural generation.

Before leaving this theme, I feel impelled to make an observation about the attitudes of Jewish communities to the Hebrew language itself. This subject is important because, historically, the attitude toward Hebrew affected attitudes toward other languages, and the degree of readiness to adopt them.

I am still unclear about the precise linguistic situation in the Palestinian Jewish community of Seleucid and early Roman times. I assume, however, that if Hebrew had still been the spoken language of Palestinian Jewry during these periods, Jews would have carried it with them everywhere and would have used it as a language of speech. This did not happen after the destruction by the Romans.

In fact, there is evidence from the Achaemenid period that Jewish colonies in Egypt used Aramaic as their language, in their own internal archives, as well as in their international correspondence. On the other hand, Isaiah 19:18 is taken to indicate that Jewish communities in Egypt spoke Canaanite, which is to say, Hebrew, during the same period. The point is that Hebrew had been on the road to restriction in the homeland, and outside it, long before the Roman destruction. It had been overtaken by Aramaic, and by a polyglot tendency which focused on Greek, especially in certain circles. I am not impressed, therefore, by the tendentious arguments of some modern Hebraists concerning the persistent loyalty of Jews to the Hebrew language. That loyalty was qualified by a tendency to restriction.

From Qumran we find the use of Aramaic to be quite rooted in the second pre-Christian century as a literary language. We now possess the Aramaic Enoch fragments, and it should be remembered that the book of Daniel, which contains extensive Aramaic sections, was finally composed in the second pre-Christian century. There is still more Aramaic material from Qumran. What this means is that the Aramaization of the Palestinian Jewish community was a pervasive phenomenon. Hebrew was restricted more and more to certain uses, consonant with a temple-centered, and school-centered, religious community. Language conflicts seem always to bear a close correlation to national feeling, and I venture to say that the restriction of Hebrew in Second Temple times was, at least in part, a response to imperial subjugation and the loss of sovereignty. Needless to say, the cognate affinity of Aramaic to Hebrew helped in its absorption.

I am surprised that the study of Aramaic is not more integral to the curriculum in Jewish studies. To this very day, it is relevant to the ethos of many Jewish communities, in diverse ways. I might also mention that in the revival of the Hebrew language, Aramaic has been indispensable. Modern Hebraists have used not only the Aramaic lexicon, but Aramaic morphology as well, in generating the neologisms so desperately required by a modern Hebraic society. As a result, contemporary Israeli Hebrew evidences a high degree of fusion.

Although Judaic classics written in Aramaic are routinely studied, I doubt whether there is an appreciation of the Aramaic universe, in the terms I have been discussing here. That can come only when language is treated as more than a key to content.

If universe and diction are important lessons to be learned from the study of language, how is language to be studied and taught in graduate programs of Jewish studies? What concerns me is the attitude, or approach to language. Language is a property, or dimension intrinsic to the materials we study. Most of the source materials we study are, after all, written in languages. The fault of the new movement in Jewish studies has been the illusion that great thoughts can be grasped, great discussions undertaken, and great movements interpreted without a deep understanding of language.

I must, however, qualify my advocacy of language study. There is certainly validity to purely linguistic study, but it seems to me that within graduate programs of Jewish studies it is best to employ scholars whose linguistic competence is complemented by a degree of knowledge of, and sensitivity to, other aspects of the course of study. I doubt whether it is necessary to sacrifice sound language training while studying source materials from other perspectives. Some years ago, I was invited to address a class in Ugaritic at a major university. The students began to murmur when I referred to the enclitic *Mem*, a major feature of the Ugaritic language. They did not know what an enclitic *Mem* is! It turned out that the class was *about* Ugaritic, but did not include a study of the language. On the graduate level, there is really no room for courses *about* anything!

In contrast, I have observed courses in Ugaritic in which almost the entire time is spent in linguistic analysis, so that students complete the course without ever becoming aware of what is written in Ugaritic. I have observed courses in which the built-in relevance of the biblical parallels is so predominant that the Ugaritic sources never speak for themselves; so that all that the student learns is the putative significance of Ugaritic to biblical studies. There is, therefore, need for a good deal of thinking and planning if language study is to accomplish its proper intent within programs of Jewish studies.

I can best propose an approach to the relevance of language by reference to the methods I have pursued in my own research, and which I have attempted to transmit in graduate instruction. Some illustrations will make the method clear.

Some years ago I contributed an appendix to the fifth volume of Jacob Neusner's *A History of the Jews in Babylonia*, entitled: "The Language of the Magical Bowls." Only a couple of years ago, I received a manuscript from an anthropologist at Tel Aviv University,

Shlomo Deshen, who found a point I had raised in my study useful for his purposes. He had undertaken to apply anthropological methodology to the solution of a problem in the history of Jewish liturgy. He sought to explain why the Geonim of Babylonia, over a period of centuries, had opposed the public recitation of the Kol Nidre in the synagogues.

In my study I had pointed out that the wording of the Kol Nidre shared technical formulas with the Aramaic magical bowls. More specifically, formulas for the annulment of vows were the same as those for the exorcism of demons, in the magical bowls. The annulment of vows is expressed as their abandonment, subjugation, release, etc. At times, it is difficult to ascertain the original context of these formulas, so pervasive are the semantic transactions, and so basic the legal, magical, and liturgical themes addressed by them.

It is Deshen's hypothesis that the Geonim objected to the public recitation of the Kol Nidre for fear that its dicta would be associated in the popular mind with the current magical amulets and bowls. At a later time, and in Europe, for the most part, these restrictions were gradually relaxed, because such associations were no longer probable.

I am not able to confirm Deshen's hypothesis, which may or may not be correct. What interests me is that a comparison of terminology was suggestive to an anthropologist, for whom it raised the possibility of social and cultural interaction.

One of the first insights of a social and historical nature I ever attained in my work on the Israelite cult pertains to the provenance of cultic terminology. It seems, upon examination, that both priestly writers and royal scribes appropriated many terms of reference from the administrative vocabulary, to be used as cultic terms. This is hardly to be wondered at, since cults operated under royal sponsorship, of one sort or another, and always did business, which required keeping accounts. In studying tablets from the great collections of temple accounts discovered in Mesopotamia and Syria I learned that in its structure, Hebrew cultic terminology was based on very ancient accounting methods and scribal conventions, just as the structure of the biblical cult itself reflected very ancient patterns of worship and sacrifice.

Although formulated at a later period, the biblical cultic texts often used administrative terms in the same way that earlier traditions had done. So, the term for the daily sacrifice, *tamid*, is, even in the Bible, a term of administrative provenance, meaning "regular allocation, daily ration." The term *minḥah* essentially means "tribute, gift," and is so used in the Bible. Aside from the semantic insight, these facts of language made it evident to me that terminology was a code, which revealed interrelationships of an institutional character between temples and other establishments within the same society.

I often find what I consider to be serious misinterpretations of documentary evidence, which can be attributed to the failure to understand ancient usage. Some years ago I prepared a study of the Aramaic inscriptions found in the treasury of Persepolis, and dating to the fifth century B.C.E. Raymond Bowman had produced an extensive edition of these inscriptions, but in examining his interpretations of them, I came to the conclusion that he had proceeded on the wrong assumption. He assumed that because the inscriptions were found on stone objects used in rituals, the inscriptions themselves were to be understood as describing those rituals. He consequently interpreted them as ritual texts, whereas my sense was that the texts themselves were of another order. In my view, they recorded the donors of the stone objects, in a manner similar to many dedicatory inscriptions and votives already known to us, in Aramaic and in other languages as well. In my opinion, Bowman had failed to take account of the transactions operative in language, and erred in his attribution of the provenance of the inscriptions.

The value of terminology is perhaps more generally recognized than that of linguistic structures, morphology, syntax, etc. This is puzzling, because so much of the progress is linguistics in recent years has been precisely in areas such as syntax. I have found morphology and syntax to be very important for cultic studies, and I wish to cite an instance of each.

In a popular study on biblical phenomenology entitled "The Language of the Holy: Perceptions of the Sacred in the Hebrew Bible," I attempt to show how different forms of the Hebrew verb *qadash* convey differing aspects of sanctification. One example will demonstrate the significance of morphology: The Segollate, *quṭl* form, *qodesh*, in Hebrew, is usually rendered "holiness." This form is the closest we come to abstraction in biblical Hebrew, and yet I have found only one limited context in which *qodesh* means "holiness" in what we would consider an abstract sense. Normally, *qodesh* will designate something holy, or a holy place. In construct formations, which gets us into syntax, it will have an adjectival sense. The only respect in which *qodesh* means holiness as an abstract quality is in the statement that God swears by his "holiness." This is similar to saying that he swears by his life, or by his faithfulness, or "by Myself"! (see Amos 4:2 with Amos 6:8 and Jeremiah 51:14).

I can account for all other occurrences of the form *qodesh* on the basis that they convey something more concrete than "holiness." Even the well-known verse in Exodus 15:11 is no exception. It is usually rendered somewhat as follows:

Who is comparable to you among the gods, LORD?
Who is comparable to you, *exalted in holiness,*
venerated in praises, doing wonders?

In this case, the poetics of biblical Hebrew suggest that the parallelism of the verse makes it likely that Massoretic *ne'dar ba-qodesh* is to be read *ba-q'doshim*, "among the deities." This would yield a closer parallelism:

Who is comparable to you among the god, LORD?
Who is comparable to you, *exalted among the deities,* etc.

Admittedly, in this instance, the text itself is problematic, but in most cases, the text as it stands suggests that abstraction was not the norm in perceptions of the holy, and that most of the time, the Hebrew Bible is describing a concrete perception, anchored in space, or substance.

In the area of syntax, I was attracted at an early point in my studies to differences between Hebrew and Akkadian syntax, which I thought could be attributed to conceptual differences. I ventured an interpretation of the pivotal verb *kipper*, "to expiate," based primarily on Akkadian evidence. The basic sense of the verb is, I maintained, not that of concealment, or "covering over" the sins, but rather that of wiping off, cleansing. There was little problem in this interpretation, except that there were syntactic differences between Akkadian and Hebrew. In Akkadian, the cognate verb *kuppuru* took the direct object, whereas Hebrew, along with retaining the direct-object syntax, also had a number of indirect-object constructions, such as *kipper ʿal, kipper bʿʿad, kipper l—*.

It was quite clear that in Hebrew, the notion of expiation being conveyed was not simply that of "wiping off" sins and impurity. The indirect-object constructions were rather conveying indirect effects, or the results of expiation. In Israelite religion, expiatory rites were addressed to God, who grants expiation. When the rituals are performed properly, and with the proper intent, expiation results; but this is so not because some impurity is actually "wiped off," necessarily, but because God had decided, as it were, to grant expiation. So, *kipper l—* means "grant 'wiping off' to—"; and *kipper bʿʿad* means: "secure 'wiping off' for—," etc.

This distinction, expressed in syntax, is corroborated by the fact that when actual wiping off or cleansing occurs, Hebrew also uses the direct-object syntax, as does Akkadian.

If language is as important as I have been claiming that it is, we should be able to derive historical insight from language. Ultimately, we should be able to learn from language something relevant to the historical reconstruction of the past.

I have recently become interested in the use of linguistic criteria in dating ancient texts. Within Torah literature, the priestly source, known as "P," has been the object of many attempts to date its contents on the basis of language. The motivation underlying this enterprise is obvious: most of what we know about the ancient cult of Israel in detail, of festival celebrations and modes of worship, is preserved in the priestly source. If we knew what historic situations are reflected in the rituals and legalities of P, we would know much more about the historical development of Israelite religion as a whole.

Classically, the debate has focused on the alternatives of preexilic, exilic, or postexilic dating, and, in linguistic terms, on the contrast between the Hebrew of the First Temple and that known from later, Second Temple times, as represented in Chronicles, for example.

More recently both I and a Canadian scholar, Robert Polzin, have argued for a middle period of literary activity among the priests, between the near-exilic period and the late exilic period represented by Chronicles; in other words, for the period up to the first mission of Nehemiah, toward the end of the fifth century.

In pursuing this course of study, I have engaged in debate with Avi Hurvitz of the Hebrew University, who argues for the preexilic provenance of the priestly writings, on linguistic grounds. Hurvitz claims that he is interested in objective, linguistic criteria, which involve no historical presuppositions. He is concerned with such phenomena as replacement, which proves a sequence from earlier to later composition. My contention has been that in studying ancient literature linguistic criteria cannot be used by themselves, without recourse to other sorts of evidence; that in the enterprise of dating there are no purely linguistic questions; that all our queries are composite, not simple.

The first intimation of postexilic vocabulary in P was use of the term *degel* in Numbers chapters 2 and 10, as a way of referring to an array of three tribes. I consider it as a replacement for the more usual term *maḥaneh*," encampment," in the biblical projection of the Israelite forces in Sinai. The most obvious provenance for the term *degel* as a sociomilitary unit (not a "banner," or the like) is in the Achaemenid period. We have contemporary, external evidence from Aramaic documents of the fifth century B.C.E., from Egypt, and now from Arad in the Negev, to indicate that this was the term used widely in the Persian imperial forces for military units stationed in the outlying provinces.

Unfortunately, the term *degel* is problematic in many ways. It is difficult to be certain that it was not used in preexilic times. It may in fact be a very old term, but it is unattested in biblical Hebrew, I maintain, before the Persian period. It is certainly not part of the lexicon of First Temple literature. It is most likely a West Semitic term which reentered the mainstream through Aramaic, as did many peripheral terms, once Aramaic became the language of the Persian empire.

I argued for the obvious: If a biblical writer wanted to portray the Israelite encampments in the Sinai, before the conquest and settlement of Canaan by the early Israelites, and chose the term *degel* to convey this portrayal, he must have written at a time when this term was in use. This brings us to the early postexilic period.

To be sure, my discussion of the term *degel*, which appeared in *Eretz-Israel* 16, a volume in honor of Harry Orlinsky, includes a thorough etymological discussion. I proceed quite quickly, however, to other considerations—the transmission of West Semitic diction via Aramaic, the cultural universe of biblical writers, and the effects of Persian imperial domination on the language of Hebrew writers.

The above illustrations of methodology were intended to argue for a different attitude toward the study of language in graduate programs of Jewish studies. My illustrations are taken from my own areas of interest, but they could be paralleled by other illustrations covering the full extent of Jewish history.

I could hardly conclude a discussion of language without mention of the modern revival of the Hebrew language as a cultural reality. The fact that the culture of modern Israel is Hebraic should have significance. I get the impression that many leaders in the field of Jewish studies remain somewhat blasé about what is a truly unique cultural phenomenon, one which is bound to affect the universe of the Jewish people. While engaged in worthwhile efforts at translation, through which we hope to present our heritage to the uninitiated among us, and to the Western world, we should not neglect our own need to experience our heritage in all its originality and vitality.

8. Graduate Education in Jewish Philosophy

Marvin Fox

In this paper I shall attempt to answer three questions. How do we define the field of Jewish philosophy? What do Ph.D.'s in Jewish philosophy have to know? What must Ph.D.'s in this field be able to do as teachers and scholars within the academic community? It should be noted that we have few models to examine or to imitate, since the number of full doctoral programs in Jewish philosophy is very limited, and in the United States the field is so young that it is only now beginning to develop consciousness of self. As a result, the views offered here are neither a report of what is being done generally, nor an account of positions commonly held by graduate teachers in the field. They are no more than the convictions of one teacher of Jewish philosophy who has been occupied in the field for many years and has supervised the doctoral training of a considerable number of students.

It is usual for discussion of our subject to begin by asking what we mean by Jewish philosophy and whether there is, in fact, such a field. The very question would be unlikely to arise if we were talking about biblical studies, rabbinics, Jewish history, or Hebrew literature. In the case of Jewish philosophy, there are those who deny that there even is such a subject. In the familiar formulation, if it is philosophy it is not Jewish, and if it is Jewish it is not philosophy. Philosophy is held to be universal, transcending particular cultures and particular times, addressing itself to basic issues which are the concern of all mankind. If philosophy has as its subject those ultimate issues which are the presuppositions of all rational thought, the foundations of all wise and virtuous action, and the ground of all sound esthetic judgment, then it seemingly cannot be confined by time, place, or culture. It would then follow that "Jewish philosophy" is a contradiction in terms.

Such purist views are, however, refuted by the actualities of the history of philosophical thought, and by the practice of scholars in the field. Despite claims that philosophy is universal, it is easy enough to show that particular philosophies are very much the product of specific cultural and historical circumstances. Greek philosophy is not simply universal philosophy which happens to be written in Greek. Plato and Aristotle are the products of their times, of a special kind of education, of thought about issues and problems which arose in their specific setting. This is clearly exemplified in a chapter of a recent book on Plato which discusses "the Greek heritage of Plato."[1] Following this tendency, writers on Greek philosophy often use such expressions as "the Greek mind." Although there is by no means universal agreement as to exactly what the main features are of "the Greek mind," it is nevertheless undeniable that Greek philosophy reflects the particular characteristics of Greek culture, the concerns and the styles of thinking of classical Greece. Scholars tend to agree, to take one example, that philosophy in Greece emerges from and is affected by mythical thinking. An important historian of Greek philosophy reminds us that "besides appreciating what is of permanent value in Greek Thought, we may also learn from observing how much latent mythology it continued to shelter within what appear to be a roof and walls of solid reason. . . . Even Aristotle, to whom in spite of his critics in all ages we owe so much of the indispensable groundwork of abstract concepts on which our thinking is based, has some fixed ideas which we encounter with a sense of shock; for example, a conviction that the heavenly bodies are living creatures, a belief in the special perfection of circularity or sphericity, and some curious notions about the primacy of the number three which clearly antedate the beginnings of philosophical thought."[2]

It should hardly be necessary to bring evidence for the very existence, to say nothing of the legitimacy, of the field which we call Jewish philosophy. If the standard criticism is applied even-handedly, then we should conclude that, if it is Greek, or German, or Anglo-American, it cannot be philosophy. No reasonable student of these matters is prepared to say that, even about so "pure" and abstract a subject as logic. The term "Roman logic" refers to an identifiable body of logic within the larger stream. Readers of contemporary philosophy have no difficulty in distinguishing Anglo-American from Continental philosophy. Each has its own characteristics, stemming from the culture out of which it comes. There is then no reason to feel uncomfortable with a body of material that we call Jewish philosophy. It exists, and it is no less philosophically interesting and legitimate than any of the other great philosophical traditions.

To speak responsibly in this forum about graduate education in Jewish philosophy, we must first provide, if not a formal definition, at least an outline of its main features. As I understand it, Jewish philosophy is systematic and critical thought carried on within the framework of Judaism. Thinkers who deal with any of the whole range of classical philosophic problems, but who do so within the religious and cultural traditions of Judaism, are doing Jewish philosophy. If they are Jews, they are seeking philosophic truth in a way which will help them in their own self-definition. They are committed to absolute and rigorous intellectual honesty, the best critical methods of which they are capable, and at the same time they are equally committed to living and thinking within the context of the Jewish faith-community. When, as in the case of Spinoza, they discard the Jewish religious framework, they may remain philosophers, but they are no longer Jewish philosophers. In turn, if they discard the demands of intellectual rigor and critical reflection which are essential to all genuine philosophy, they may continue to be faithful Jews, but they are no longer philosophers. The types are not, in general, difficult to identify. Saadia, Maimonides, Hermann Cohen are Jewish philosophers. Spinoza, Bergson, Husserl are philosophers who are (or once were) Jews. Jews who are not philosophers at all are so common a type that they need not be named.

The subject matter of Jewish philosophy includes as its most readily identifiable content the main works of the most important Jewish philosophers. These constitute the central core of the literature of the field. We shall later consider what is involved in training graduate students to master these materials. I would argue, however, that the character of these very works leads us to an expanded conception of the subject matter of Jewish philosophy, one that includes a great deal more than technical philosophic studies. Jewish philosophers are often deeply influenced by non-Jewish philosophical traditions, but their Jewish interest and value depend on the way in which they deal with the materials of the Jewish tradition. That Philo was influenced by earlier Greek philosophy, Saadia by Kalam, Maimonides by Aristotle and certain Islamic thinkers, Hermann Cohen by Kant, is not in dispute. This is why one of our main tasks in graduate education in Jewish philosophy is to make certain that our students have, or acquire, the general philosophic background without which they cannot properly master their materials. This, however, is only one side of the story. Jewish philosophers without exception draw heavily on biblical and rabbinic sources. They turn both to *halakha* and *aggada*. They build their philosophic account of Judaism on the foundations of classical and Jewish literature. This literature, its ideas and its doctrines, forms the basis for their philosophic activity. It follows that the subject matter of Jewish philosophy must be seen as including that entire literature to the extent that it is philosophically relevant.

A competent student of Jewish philosophy must know well the main movements and works of Western thought which have influenced Jewish philosophers in each period. He must have not only general philosophic knowledge, but also the intellectual skills of the philosopher. He must be acute in argument, sharp in analysis, a careful reader of difficult texts, and one who can effectively synthesize and systematize bodies of complex philosophic materials. In addition, it goes without saying that he must achieve a thorough knowledge of the main works of Jewish philosophy of all historical periods. As we have shown, this, in turn, presupposes a high level of competence in dealing with the Bible and rabbinic literature.

What are the objectives of graduate education in this field? The initial set of objectives is defined by the subject matter which we expect the student to master. First, and most important, our students must be trained to do philosophy and to approach our materials with philosophic insight and sophistication. This may seem obvious, but it is not. An inordinate amount of work in the field of Jewish philosophy has been done by historians and philologists. They make useful contributions to the background which is required for dealing with Jewish philosophical texts, but this is no substitute for the philosophical work itself. As a practical matter in the present setting of graduate studies in Jewish philosophy, we daily confront students who have not had sound philosophical training. Either we must refuse to accept into our doctoral programs any student who has not had thorough general training in philosophy, or we must be prepared to provide that training as part of a graduate program in Jewish philosophy. Whichever way we choose to go, it is axiomatic that we cannot train credible Ph.D.'s in Jewish philosophy without requiring of them demonstrated philosophical ability. We serve no useful purpose by multiplying the numbers of those who will continue to write about topics in Jewish philosophy in ways that are philosophically incompetent.

We must, therefore, make certain first that our students have a mastery of logic, both classical and modern. They need not be outstanding specialists in the field, unless that is the area of their particular interest. However, they must be able to follow the course of an argument, to distinguish premises from conclusions, to formalize an argument so that it can be critically understood and evaluated. In brief, they must be able to use the techniques of the logician as a necessary condition of gaining sound insight into the philosophies that they are studying. In general philosophical studies this is so much taken for granted that it would seem odd even to mention it. In Jewish philosophical studies such logical care and rigor is by no means the accepted norm. Arguments are stated and repeated. Their history may be traced, and the terms which are used may be examined both historically and philosophically. Rarely, however, does one find anyone who asks whether the premises are true and whether the argument is sound. But this is the place where the philosophic work begins, and to carry out this work competently one needs to have a reasonably good mastery of logic. Lest this seem like a radical demand to anyone who knows the state of current work in Jewish philosophy, we would do well to remember that control of logic was among the first prerequisites which Maimonides set for any student of his *Guide of the Perplexed*.

Let us consider just two examples to illustrate the point. Saadia is usually credited with having introduced into Jewish philosophy the notion of "rational commandments." The claim that there are rational commandments is, on the face of it, extremely important. Yet, hardly anyone has asked what Saadia means by the term "rational" in this usage. The question is, in part, a purely logical one. If he means what logicians normally mean by "rational" when they speak of an argument as rational, then he is making a very strong claim. He would then be saying that just as in the use of a rational argument the conclusion follows necessarily from the premises, so in the case of rational commandments does our reason teach us that these rules of behavior are absolutely binding. On the other hand, if he means by "rational" no more than "reasonable," "prudent," "useful" or the like, his claim is of a quite different order. The question is first and foremost one that requires logical analysis for its resolution. A reader who is ignorant of logic, or who does not automatically think of issues in logic when he studies such materials, will never even raise the question, much less resolve it.[3] A logical analysis of terms and the arguments in which they are used is required.

Maimonides provides us with another kind of example in his extended treatment of the question whether the world is eternal or created. There are two features to his argument. First, he wants to show that while Aristotle believed in the eternity of the world, he never provided a demonstrative argument in favor of his thesis. Maimonides claims that Aristotle presented us only with arguments from probability, and these were, in Maimonides' opinion, not even good probability arguments. Second, Maimonides proposes the thesis that the question itself is, in principle, incapable of solution either by demonstration or by sound inductive arguments. No one can understand this long discussion in the *Guide* without proper training in logic. One must know a good deal about probability and induction in order to be able to do a precise logical analysis of the Aristotelian materials and of Maimonides' restatement of Aristotle. Similarly, one must have a high level of logical sophistication in order to deal with the claim that this question is, in principle, not soluble in a way that is philosophically sound. If Maimonides is right, then there is considerable merit in his view that the creation/eternity question must be settled on nonphilosophical grounds. If he is wrong, then, by his own admission, a major cornerstone of Jewish faith has been destroyed. Simple paraphrases of the text will not do. The subject demands rigorous logical analysis.

Logic, however, is only a formal tool. Although it is indispensable for any serious philosophic work, it has no philosophic content of its own. For this reason a properly trained student of Jewish philosophy must also have a sophisticated control of metaphysics, epistemology, and ethics. The literature of Jewish philosophy contains a variety of metaphysical, epistemological, and ethical theories. Some are largely taken over from earlier philosophers, while others are original with the Jewish writers. In either case a reader who approaches these texts with a simple-minded grasp of these subjects is doomed to a totally inadequate understanding.

Consider, for example, the many studies of Buber which do little more than repeat in inelegant paraphrases some of his striking language, but which never confront with the tools of philosophical analysis the metaphysical problems that he poses. Let us simply look briefly at two statements in *I and Thou* which are as characteristic of Buber's thought as almost anything that he wrote.

> Of course, God is "The wholly other"; but he is also the wholly same: the wholly present. Of course, he is the *mysterium tremendum* that appears and overwhelms; but he is also the mystery of the obvious that is closer to me than my own I.[4]

> Yes, in the pure relationship you felt altogether dependent, as you could never possibly feel in any other—and yet also altogether free as never and nowhere else; created—and creative. You no longer felt the one, limited by the other; you felt both without bonds, both at once.
> That you need God more than anything, you know at all times in your heart. But don't you know also that God needs you—in the fulness of his eternity, you?[5]

These statements, if they are to be taken seriously, raise a whole series of metaphysical and epistemological questions. One wants to suppose that Buber meant something important when he wrote these words, that they are not mere rhetorical bombast. If this is philosophy, not poetry, then the serious reader must subject these statements to careful metaphysical unpacking and analysis. What is meant by referring to God as both wholly other and simultaneously wholly same? Is this some sort of Hegelian metaphysic, Kierkegaardian paradox, or what? Will we be able to settle the matter by a careful study of the entire book in which these statements are contained, or must we go outside to other philosophic sources? In any case, no one innocent of metaphysics will even be sensitive to the issues, much less capable of resolving them.

The claim that "you know at all times in your heart" that you need God more than anything poses an epistemological challenge. What kind of knowledge is this knowledge in one's heart? Is it verifiable? Is it, as Buber seems to claim, universal human knowledge, and if so where is the evidence for it? These are not minor textual quibbles; they are questions which go to the very heart of our understanding of Buber's thought. Unless the student of modern Jewish philosophy addresses such texts with all the sophistication of the trained student of metaphysics and epistemology, he will never achieve clarity about Buber's meaning. He will certainly never be able to provide his own explicatory account of Buber, and will have no ground for evaluating Buber's contribution to Jewish religious philosophy. A well-trained student of philosophy does not simply worship at the shrine of a great thinker. His task is to understand critically, to reflect, to reconstruct, and to evaluate. Without this work he will never be able to judge whether Buber or any other Jewish thinker is philosophically sound and serious or whether he is Jewishly authentic.

If the first objective of graduate education in Jewish philosophy is to make certain that the student has sound general philosophical training and skills, the second objective is to make certain that he is appropriately equipped to deal with the specifically Jewish dimension of the works of Jewish philosophers. This requires that he have, as we have already noted, a sound grasp of works of classical Jewish literature, i.e., Bible, Talmud, Midrash, etc. Unless that world is open to the student he will have no way of understanding and judging the uses which the philosophers make of these sources. It may be too much to ask that each graduate student in Jewish philosophy have had a deep and thorough classical Jewish education, although this is certainly most desirable. What is indispensable is a level of familiarity with the classical materials which enables the student to react with critical intelligence to the philosophic use and philosophic transformation of the classical sources.

Consider a case. Maimonides claims that scripture is to be read figuratively whenever necessary so as to make it accord with independent philosophic truth. Is this a sound way to read scripture? Is it

Graduate Education in Jewish Philosophy 129

a Jewishly legitimate way? No one can begin to answer these questions who does not know a good deal about the Bible and about classical Jewish ways of reading the Bible. In certain arguments in which he cites scriptural proof texts, Maimonides chooses obscure and unfamiliar verses while ignoring those which might be known to any minimally educated Jew. If the student of Jewish philosophy does not have at least a basic classical Jewish education, he will not even be aware that Maimonides has done something strange. Without that awareness he can neither confront nor resolve the problem posed by these unusual selections. From Philo to Hermann Cohen and Martin Buber, the use of scripture by Jewish philosophers presents a major challenge to the critical understanding and judgment of serious students of their works. The same can be said of the use made by these philosophers of Talmudic and *midrashic* materials, in fact of the entire range of "official" Jewish literature. As in the case of general philosophic knowledge, we can either make an appropriate level of Jewish knowledge an absolute prerequisite for admission to our doctoral programs, or we can try to remedy the deficiency of those who come with insufficient preparation in classical Jewish learning. What is certain is that we cannot properly train students in Jewish philosophy if they are seriously deficient in their knowledge of the classical sources of Judaism.

The initial objectives of graduate education in Jewish philosophy have been stated in terms of preparation for scholarship in the field. To the mastery of Jewish classical literature and general philosophy we should add, of course, proper control of the requisite languages. For serious philosophic work, however, scholarship is a necessary, but not a sufficient condition. We should be training our students not only to master the literature of our philosophic past, but also to do their own creative philosophic work in the present. We should help and encourage them to do philosophy and not only to be well-trained philosophic scholars. Then they may use their knowledge of the existing literature in the field not only to teach but also to contribute valuable historical, philological, or philosophically interpretive studies of the works of earlier philosophers. As against the philosophic scholar, the philosopher will address Jewish philosophic issues anew, not only as a student of the work of others but as an original contributor to thought in this field.

The creative work of Jewish philosophy did not end with Buber,

Rosenzweig, and Heschel, nor is it coming to an end in the work of Soloveitchik and Kaplan. The task is ongoing, and no generation that takes Judaism seriously can ignore it. We must confront the old issues in the context of contemporary thought; otherwise we shall have a Judaism for antiquarians, but not for contemporary man. We must ask, how shall a Jew think and talk about God today? What can revelation and redemption mean to us? Our culture is that of modern science, just as Maimonides' culture was that of the then-current versions of Aristotelian philosophy. We need to face the philosophic problems of Judaism in our own setting and with our own creative philosophical energies. It is much safer to stick only to an interpretation of the old texts, much safer and much less demanding. Philosophic originality cannot be taught in the way in which we can teach students to explicate a text. Nor does every student, even if very bright, have the gifts for philosophic originality. Yet, if the training we offer, and the models we present, do nothing to stimulate that originality where the capacity for it does exist, we shall not produce even one new insight in Jewish philosophy out of all our schools. The natural and social sciences, the art and the literature of our century challenge us forcefully to new reflection on the perennial problems of a philosophic understanding of Judaism. The breakdown of traditional morality forces us to confront religioethical questions. We can expect to gain help and illumination from a careful study of the philosophic work of our predecessors. Plato will always be relevant to contemporary work in general philosophy, and Maimonides will always be relevant to contemporary work in Jewish philosophy, but neither of them can do our work for us. They expand our insights and understanding. They provide superb models for us of how to go about philosophizing in our own setting. But we have as our academic obligation the responsibility to go forward with the actual work of Jewish philosophy today.

The training of students so as to open them up to independent thought on these matters should consist of two elements. First, we should help them read the great works of the past as living documents, rather than as dead texts through which they plod obediently in order to pass a set of examinations. For our students to learn to do philosophy, not merely to learn about it, they must come to understand and participate in the living philosophic reality of great works of the past. An intense effort of imaginative self-transcendence is required in order to achieve this goal. We must read Philo or Maimonides as if we were their contemporaries, facing their problems in the context of their cultures. How else can one come to know the inner character of the creative work done by these great minds? We too often tend to teach philosophy as if the texts had an independent life of their own, forgetting that they were written by living men who had problems that they were trying to solve. We cannot train our students to do their own independent philosophic work unless we help them to see what our great predecessors were doing and how they did it. Once they come to recognize this, they may be somewhat less reticent about their own attempts at solving contemporary philosophic issues. Contrary to the popular hymn which asserts that "that old-time religion is good enough for me," we are arguing that the old-time religion can live intellectually only if it undergoes a philosophic renewal in each generation. The medievals were concerned with creation versus eternity, while we must be concerned with creationism versus evolution. The medievals were concerned with the status of the divine commandments in the light of a rational natural moral law. We are concerned with the status of absolute divine commandments in the light of an almost total moral relativism. In each area of religious thought we are similarly confronted by the specific problematic of our own time. The Jewish philosopher is forced to address the old questions anew. He cannot rest with historical learning alone, however deep and subtle it may be.

There is an additional dimension of philosophic creativity for which we should be training our students. I refer to the reading of classical nonphilosophical Jewish texts so as to extract from them their philosophic elements. This is work which has hardly begun. Yet it represents one of the major untapped resources for Jewish philosophical thought. It attaches our thinking to the sources of our past and makes those works speak effectively to us in the present.

What I am proposing is nothing less than the recovery of the literature of *aggada* and *halakha* for Jewish philosophical thought. One hardly has to make the obvious point that this literature is not a body of systematic philosophy, but it does not follow that there is nothing in these materials of philosophic interest and importance. What is needed is the development of the sensitivities which will find and respond to those philosophically interesting elements which have almost totally been neglected until now. We have a model in the work of the major Jewish philosophers. They frequently showed us how to read a *midrash* in ways which are philosophically illuminating. But these philosophers did not set themselves the task of producing a philosophical account of the entire corpus of *midrash*. They simply selected those passages which were useful or interesting to them in order to sustain particular arguments or to make specific points. What I am proposing is that part of our current philosophic work must include an appropriate philosophic examination of the entire body of *midrashic* and *halakhic* materials. Not all of it will prove to be interesting, but there is overwhelming evidence that there is much treasure to be dug up here.

Yonah Frankel, an Israeli scholar, has recently published a book which opens up in a preliminary way some of the issues in this field.[6] From the few cases with which he deals he can see that *midrashic* texts deal with such problems as human free will and God's foreknowledge; the relationship between a fixed order of nature and miracles; death, and immortality; and other philosophic subjects. From his small sample it is evident that a philosophic study of *midrashic* materials would pay rich rewards in deepening Jewish thought and anchoring it more firmly to the classical sources. We must train our students to read *midrash* with an eye for its philosophic significance. Teachers of Jewish philosophy will have to create the models and the methods because so little exists currently in this field.

It is no less important to train students to read the *halakhic* literature philosophically. The greatest effort of Jewish intellectual activity over many centuries went into the *halakha*. Our colleague, Jacob Neusner, has done pioneering work in uncovering the theoretical world view of the Mishnah. We can no longer have any doubt that Mishnah does have such a world view, nor is there much reason to doubt that the same is true of later *halakhic* works. Neusner would be the first to admit that while his work has opened the doors, much still remains to be done. Jewish philosophy has as one of its tasks picking up and continuing this work. We need to study and explicate the ethics of the *halakha*, or at least to determine whether the very notion of ethics in the *halakha* makes any sense. We need to uncover the conceptions of man and society that underlie major *halakhic* treatises. We must try to formulate some clear account of the conceptions of God which are present in the various treatises of the *halakha*. These are only a few of the topics which need investigation. There is a whole body of Jewish philosophic work waiting to be done here. Training our graduate students for this work should be among our prime objectives.

Finally, we must be concerned with the place of Jewish philosophy in the general humanistic curriculum. Our setting is the university, not the seminary or the *yeshiva*. We see our work as integrally related to the larger context of university education, and we must determine the ways in which our subject is properly part of the university. If our students are to function effectively as university teachers in their own field, they must have a larger vision of that field within the university. This is not the place to develop a complete theory of that relationship, but we certainly can point out some of its features. We take it for granted that in a university work in Jewish philosophy flows out of the general intellectual setting of which we are a part. This means that we do not presume to do our studies in isolation from our own academic culture in general, or in isolation from the work of our colleagues in immediately related fields. We cannot be detached from contemporary currents in general philosophy. We must be informed by the best work in intellectual history. As our literary colleagues develop their studies in methods of textual explication and in the problems of interpretation, we must know what they are doing and see its possible significance for our own philosophic work. The same can be said for developments in legal theory and legal history and for any number of other areas in the social sciences. In turn, we have the heavy responsibility of making the academy aware of the general significance of our Jewish materials. Our task is to engage neither in apologetics nor in a kind of chauvinistic expansionism. It is simply to make Jewish learning what it properly ought to be in the university, a valued partner in the common intellectual enterprise. I do not believe that there is any formal way to train our students to take part in this effort. It will not be achieved by an additional course or by some other formal device. We can only exemplify for them by our own conduct within the university what it means for Jewish scholarship to live in a creative symbiosis with the rest of the academy.

It should be clear that no existing program of graduate study in Jewish philosophy actually achieves all the objectives which have been set forth in this paper. No program can hope to do it all, nor can any one student be expected to master it all. Even while we hope that our students will exceed their teachers in learning and in creative scholarly achievement, our sense of reality tells us that no one individual among them is likely to become the perfect model of the Jewish philosopher. If there is any merit to this set of proposals, it is that it opens the way for individual programs to determine what they can do and what they want to do, to choose what role they intend to play in the training of students in Jewish philosophy. Students should know what to expect from each particular program and should be able to select in accordance with their own interests. However, no program which presumes to offer responsible doctoral studies in this field can afford to ignore completely any of the elements which have been outlined here. Some acquaintance with and competence in each of these areas are necessary for sound work in Jewish philosophy. Individual scholars and university programs must determine where their interests lead them and what their strengths are. They should attempt no more than they can do honestly and well. Yet, they cannot give sound training in Jewish philosophy, in my opinion, unless they are open to and concerned with the range of issues and objectives outlined in this paper.

Notes

1 John Herman Randall, *Plato: Dramatist of the Life of Reason* (New York & London, 1970), chap. 4.
2 W. K. C. Guthrie, *A History of Greek Philosophy* (Cambridge, 1967), Vol. 1, pp. 1, 2.
3 For a discussion of this issue, see M. Fox, "On the Rational Commandments in Saadia," *Modern Jewish Ethics: Theory and Practice*, ed. M. Fox (Ohio State University Press, 1975).
4 Martin Buber, *I and Thou*, trans. Walter Kaufmann (New York, 1970), p. 127.
5 Ibid., p. 130.
6 Yonah Frankel, *Iyyunim Beʿolamo Haruhani shel Sippur Haʾaggadah* (Hakibbutz Hameuchad, 1981).

9. Graduate Studies in Jewish History

Marc Lee Raphael

Introduction

It is difficult to gain perspective on graduate education. We who are in it lack distance from it, but we also lack the help of outside critics. Everyone feels free to criticize elementary education; a few confidently can level their barbs at college education; but who is there to criticize graduate education except those who are in it? Without distance and objective criticism, it is difficult to acquire leverage on one's perceptions in order to pry them loose for examination and reorientation. But though gaining perspective is difficult, it is obviously necessary.

I view the fundamental problem of training graduate students to be the disposition of students to conform with professorial ways of thinking and teaching. As research approaches, at least within history, are subdivided into "schools of thought" and adhered to tenaciously, there is a delicate balance between not knowing enough and forging ahead on one's own, between my desire to propagate a view and the student's groping toward his/her own. Do I tend to grant students the right to originality only after they know "enough," or do I begin to encourage their acquisition of knowledge and scholarly independence as soon as they formulate questions of their own? Do I encourage their passivity vis-à-vis my field's subject matter by creating a situation where they are told what to write for their dissertation and hence dull their earliest act of serious investigation? The habit of originality does not develop after a period of obedience, and as I discuss with you the several areas of our history program I hope to constantly keep in mind the challenges inherent in the student-mentor relationship.

The Field

The field of Jewish history, as presented by doctoral students at Ohio State University, encompasses either ancient-medieval or early modern-modern Jewish history, or both. The two common denominators of both fields are the responsibility of the student to master the major Jewish historians—from antiquity to our own time—who have formulated conceptions of the Jewish past, and to articulate an understanding of both the history of Judaism as well as the history of the Jewish people. Beyond these fundamentals, the student is directed toward the basic primary and secondary sources in various periods of the Jewish past, for learning how to do research, with supervision, underlies every program in the department.

Beginning with the biblical historians, continuing with Josephus, rabbinic Judaism, and the middle ages, and then abundantly from the sixteenth century to the present, people such as Krochmal, Geiger, Graetz, Dubnow, Kaufmann, Mahler, and Baron have presented systematic philosophies of Jewish history—sometimes emphasizing the history of Judaism and sometimes emphasizing the people who developed and carried the ideas and values of Judaism.

The study of such historians—especially those who have produced multivolumed histories of the "Jewish people"—also provides us with the opportunity to address, with the student, a two-sided question. What constitutes the "Jewishness" of the Jewish people, both in any particular context of the Jewish past as well as between one discrete period and another in the entire sweep of that history? And to what extent ought one to speak of this entity as a "people?" Why, in other words, does Dubnow write about both Pharisaic Judaism and American Judaism in the same history? Is there, in fact, as Graetz, Dubnow, and Baron take for granted, a collective entity that from the sixth century B.C. to the present we are justified in calling a "people," and what constitutes their Jewishness?

One's own historical methodology in general and understanding of Jewish history in particular, we have found, are best developed by analyzing how others have conceptualized the structure of Jewish history and the history of Judaism. Even if, as Neusner has often argued, these conceptualizations of Jewish history are more historicistic theology than historiography, they are important attempts to search for that elusive thread of continuity, or constant, which encompasses the Jewish historical experience.

Together with each student, the medieval and/or modern Jewish historian tries to establish some sort of periodization, or temporal framework, within which the students might organize their studies and preparation for the doctoral examination. Such divisions are never satisfactory, primarily because the Jews have lived in so many different places—hence under such vastly different conditions—at the same time. Equally unsatisfactory, but often used in our program, in an attempt to combine, within the permitted parameters of a history department, a study of both Jews and Judaism, is a topical division, so that instead of preparing early modern and modern Jewish history the student might present five fields. These might include, for example, messianic and sectarian movements (in which, whether in the guise of socialism or Zionism, the same symbols, myths, and questions which informed Hassidism and Sabbateanism are phrased in secular ways by usually nonreligious Jews); anti-semitism and its responses; expulsion, migration, and adjustment; the religious response to modernity; and emancipation and Enlightenment/Haskalah. Whether by temporal divisions or themes, the students then take courses and read widely in the major texts and analyses of the discrete histories of the Jews and Judaism.

Thus, when a student finishes preparing for the candidacy examination, he or she should have a broad view of the entire scope of Jewish history—as gleaned from those who have written such histories—an understanding of the interpretation of the past which informs these histories, and a thorough grasp of the basic literature written during and about the several centuries of Jewish life the student has selected to emphasize.

The Course Work

Specialization has obvious merits. It gives the student a sense of competency in an area, such as the modern Jewish experience, that is the student's own "turf." And surely part of scientific progress has been due to the diversification of specialties and subspecialties. Yet there is a tendency to mine the same academic vein long after it has ceased to produce much fresh knowledge. Each discipline tends to be characterized by its own set of assumptions, jargon, models for conducting research, and, in general, its own approach to thinking about and solving problems. It is rare for graduate departments at Ohio State University to encourage their students to enroll in courses in other disciplines (with the possible exception of the cognate area in some fields), and in many departments any deviation from a rigidly prescribed course of study may result in questions about how serious the student is about a chosen field. Such a situation seems to me, and to many graduate students, unfortunate and unwise. More likely than not, such narrow academic parochialism produces researchers who are skillful technicians and masters of method, but who are inclined to pursue answers to unduly restricted questions.

The history department has attempted to respond to this tension between depth and breadth. Its depth is demonstrated by maintaining, for the past fourteen years, two Jewish historians, a medievalist and modernist, who share fourteen graduate-level courses all listed in the university catalogue. To encourage breadth, the department has strongly encouraged students to choose one of their four fields outside of history. The typical Jewish history doctoral student prepares one field in Jewish history, two in related areas of history, and one in another department. The challenge, of course, is for the student to explain to people outside the field of Jewish history, but attuned to problems of common interest, what he/she is studying. The rewards have been greater encouragement of the theoretical and generalizing propensities of future researchers, more questioning and rethinking of the concepts underlying findings and methodology, and possibly more emphasis upon imagination and creative speculation—for it appears that an important way to stimulate the theoretical capacity of students in history is by acquainting them with fields different from their own. The students have been introduced to the different assumptions and approaches of other disciplines, and this has allowed them to break out of the tight, somewhat constricting network of human relationships within their own academic department. This is somewhat parallel to my insistence that they spend time with my colleagues and hence minimize the exclusivity of their relationship with me.

This breadth has another advantage. The students are not only encouraged to touch base with the formal orientations of other disciplines, as set forth in their courses, but also to meet graduate students in other disciplines, to learn how they think, and to have the assumptions of their field questioned by those in others. There is no persuasive reason why history graduate students should spend their academic and social hours with students in their own discipline. They must, of course, pursue a necessarily specialized graduate program, requiring a certain number of seminars, but there is no need to make that graduate experience more narrow than either the students care for or we think is good for the cause of scholarship.

The number of seminars, of course, is not nearly as significant as the content of a student's program. By the end of the second quarter of doctoral work, the student and adviser now must assemble the prospective examining committee—let us say the Jewish historians, a German historian, a Russian historian, and an American historian; or the Jewish historians, a historian of religions, a French historian, and the Jewish philosophy professor—and present to the committee (and gain its approval of) the proposed course of study. Obviously changes in seminars will take place, and the early modern French historian may actually examine the candidate because the modernist has a leave, but the program of study must satisfy a group of colleagues who often feel Jewish history is rather narrow and two Jewish historians who both feel their courses are absolutely essential for an understanding of the discipline or an introduction to the profession. The strength of the program, thus, is that a student studying modern Judaism, for example, has someone in American religion and someone in the history of religions, in addition to a Jewish historian, with whom to work; the weakness is that there is always the danger that with so much breadth the amount of depth may not be sufficient. Put differently: the strength of our Jewish history organizational pattern is that a candidate will be well prepared to teach introductory survey courses in European or American civilization in another history department, but less able to offer a "Jewish studies" course—"Introduction to the Talmud" or "Mishnaic Hebrew"—far removed from the area of Jewish history the student prepares. Some depth in Judaica is obviously traded for breadth in history.

The Dissertation

The conduct of research in graduate programs seems to be based on the reasonable principle that the student learns by doing. First, students must become familiar with a body of knowledge. They then react to the material in part by evaluating the processes by which it was developed, and by making judgments about the significance of the knowledge in terms of its relevance to current issues. As a result of this review, the student then proceeds to develop a design for studying the issue, conducts the appropriate research, evaluates the data resulting from this research, and draws conclusions from the data. It is expected that these conclusions will result in the significant revision or refinement of current understandings of the issue. As a result of this experience the student presumably learns how to evaluate data, how to state the issue precisely, and how to limit his/her observations to the issue. We say that the student has learned to become a disciplined scholar capable of working independently to analyze new data, discriminating fact from fiction and significant facts from insignificant facts. We also hold that the student has made a significant contribution to knowledge in the process.

While I am not completely satisfied with this dissertation procedure, the result of adhering for nearly a century to the vision of Hermann von Helmholtz that "every student should add at least one brick to the ever growing temple of knowledge," I have generally adhered to its assumptions.[1] Nevertheless, some of my objections to this neat package have influenced my direction of theses and especially dissertations.

First, I have become acutely aware that my former students do not differ greatly from the national portrait of postdissertation research, or at least research which results in publication. A 1975 nationwide survey of faculty members in American colleges and universities revealed that:

> over half of all full-time faculty members have never written or edited any sort of book alone or in collaboration with others . . . more than one-third have never published an article . . . half of

the professorate have not published anything, or had anything accepted for publication, in the last two years . . . more than one-quarter of all full-time academics have never published a scholarly work. . . . In all, about one-fourth of the academics have published extensively—which we have construed as ten or more articles or three or more monographs. Half don't publish at all; the remaining fourth fall into the "moderate" range of publications.[2]

Secondly, I have tried to remain sensitive to the continual criticism directed at the dubious value of much dissertation research in history.[3] There are an infinite number of topics in the modern Jewish experience never studied, but whenever I begin to guide a student in the search for originality in Jewish studies I remember the words of Louis Rubin, written twenty years ago in the *American Scholar:* "[Originality] as often as not means that the student is supposed to select a topic so specialized and unimportant that even previous writers of dissertations have neglected it."[4]

The lesson to be learned from the survey and the choice of topics is that one must be careful not to make truly major claims for the dissertation. I surely hope my students come face to face with the messy and lonely business we call "research," and gain some preparation for a life of critical review and intellectual regeneration, adaption, and growth, but I must honestly say that not many of the dissertations I have directed have represented "a significant contribution to knowledge." Perhaps my students are not unique; one prominent critic of graduate education, Robert Paul Wolff, claims that if we really insist that dissertations contain truly original contributions to knowledge, then universities, on the average, would probably not grant more than two Ph.D.'s in a decade.[5]

Third, I know that, with so much at stake, the dissertation experience can be deleterious to the student-scholar's work and psyche, can even retard instead of facilitate the individual's development. In my own career as a graduate student, which began in a Jewish history department overseas, the students, and especially the faculty, spent inordinate amounts of time debunking the work of their American colleagues and almost all their predecessors. This had the effect upon me of setting impossibly high standards, and I quickly felt that my work would have to be that of a near-genius. Ideally, graduate students should be encouraged to regard the dissertation as an exercise in professional craftsmanship that will allow them to display their full originality when they rewrite it and expand it for publication—though of course the adviser must balance this reasonable expectation with the awareness that if the student lands in an unpropitious academic milieu or none at all, that opportunity may be foreclosed.

I hope my students leave with the self-confidence that one can do something hard because one already has. If one has learned a difficult foreign language, it is easier to learn another; if one has learned how to run one basic computer program, one will not be stumped when the need for another arises. When one has pursued a graduate program of breadth as well as depth, and takes his/her first job, perhaps every moment need not be spent getting up new courses—often at the introductory level—little related to one's dissertation specialty or even area of expertise. One may even be a bit less overwhelmed by the initial years of teaching and less likely to become the captive of the institution of first instance for sheer lack of time and energy to pursue one's own research.

Fourth, I remain concerned with the ultimate, or at least long-range, goal of the dissertation experience. Ann Heiss, in the *Journal of Higher Education,* reported that "activities leading to the culmination of the dissertation requirements such as the selection of a topic, the preparation of a prospectus, the collection, ordering, and analysis of data, and the actual writing of the dissertation contributed more than any other experience to the development of the doctoral respondents" in her study of over 3,000 professors in ten major universities. But I would still ask (she does not), "development" for what? To be prolific producers of esoteric refinements to existing knowledge? To be productive developers of new models and new perspectives for evaluating and dealing with the universe of experience? To be effective interpreters and teachers of existing knowledge? Her conclusion, cited above, though it appears to emerge so strongly from the "hard" data of survey responses, actually obscures the continuing need for evaluation of the place of the dissertation in the education of Ph.D. candidates.[6]

My tentative decision has been to constantly keep in mind the fact that graduate students have spent many years as students before they arrive at the graduate level and that their experiences differ greatly. Thus, I have tried to draw a careful diagnosis of the student's undergraduate education and then, together with the student and the committee I described above, design a graduate program of study, including dissertation research, especially for him or her. Fortunately, I am not so burdened by numbers that individual programming for graduate students is out of the question.

Fifth, and finally, the research and writing of a dissertation are, quite properly, a lonely endeavor in which students, through increased self-reliance, build the independent, critical, evaluative skills which are so essential to the "sifting and winnowing" upon which all real scholarship rests. Nevertheless, the adviser's role is crucial, though not so easily agreed upon. Should the adviser assign or even suggest (my usual procedure) the topic? How are differences between adviser and advisee to be resolved? How closely—intellectually and even physically—should the dissertation be supervised? I struggle constantly with these questions; but at the same time I do not hesitate to insist that graduate students share their dissertation-in-progress with each other. My experience has been that to the extent that students learn to criticize each other's work, they will also learn what to look for in their own. My role has evolved from the unquestioned, or questionable, authority from whom students must accept comments because they are backed by the power to give grades, to a participant in a group project. Now my contribution is to try to deepen the debate, to introduce insights which may have been overlooked, to suggest technical tools and sources with which the students may not as yet be familiar. It seems to me that the sharing of a dissertation-in-progress maximizes the very spirit of education—helping students to realize their own potentialities, letting them discover what they really can do, not in imitation, not in response to command, not because it has been charted for them, but because they have acquired a new view of themselves and their capacity.[7]

The Teaching Business

Teaching can be defined by its many purposes and modes. The purposes include helping students to develop the skills of recovery, articulation, and inquiry; to achieve subject matter competence;

then to transform that competence into knowledge—in sum, helping students to learn how to think and become participants in learning. The most conventional modes are formal classroom meetings in which some combination of lecture and discussion is prevalent, and they are sometimes supplemented by the use of technology—aids such as 16 mm films, tapes, and so on. Teaching often also takes place informally in professorial offices, in committees, and over meals. And surely teaching entails more than a faculty member's personal interactions with students: refining an old course, developing a new one, restructuring graduate requirements and curriculum are related to teaching. But the fundamental questions concern how one teaches, what, to whom, and why.[8]

Ideally, the students turned out by history departments with freshly minted doctorates should be equipped and trained not just to teach but to teach well. My general sense is that this ideal is rarely achieved. As far as I can discover, graduate departments rarely explicitly consider applicants' teaching potentials. According to the catalogs of the most prestigious departments, including Chicago, Harvard, Princeton, Yale, and Michigan, the stated objective of graduate instruction in history is to train both researchers and teachers. Yet not one appears to offer any kind of formal teacher-training program, and teaching assistantships, if they exist, are either mentioned briefly or described in the general comments on the graduate school as a whole.

My own experience at UCLA suggests that once students have been admitted to a graduate program, they may occasionally be in a position to display some of the qualities associated with good teaching (articulateness, clarity of thought and organization, patience, resilience), but their continuation in the program will not be contingent on displaying such qualities in teaching, nor will they be evaluated in terms of their potential as a teacher. Neither the capacity to teach, nor any demonstration of the ability to teach, is a requirement for the M.A. or Ph.D. degree. The motto at UCLA seemed to be: "If he is good enough to study history in our department, he is good enough to teach it in yours."

Many idealistic faculty emerge with Ph.D.'s determined to be teachers first of all. Though they have often been teaching assistants, they quickly recognize that they have not learned much about teaching; however, like college teachers generally, they assume that to do well at teaching is a matter of will and desire. The truth, of course, is that good teaching is as exacting as good research (though ordinary teaching, protected by the privacy of the classroom, is perhaps not as arduous as ordinary research), and the mandate "teach or perish" is more imperious and destructive than the better-known maxim "publish or perish."

What then do I try to provide to enable my students to learn how to teach? First, it can be argued with some validity that most of the academic activities engaged in by graduate students contribute in some way to the development of their teaching abilities. Perceptive students will almost automatically evaluate the organization, structure, and content of their courses, analyze the reasons for the courses' successes and failures, and, of course, gain much from seminar presentations. Such benefits should not be gainsaid. Yet, although good teaching may be a necessary prerequisite to the production of good teachers by example, it is not sufficient. The students have not gone through the process of designing and teaching a course with a faculty member or by themselves. They have had no conscious instruction and systematic discussion of the factors involved in teaching: articulating specific course objectives and designing a syllabus to meet these; explaining the rationale for exams and paper requirements; justifying the mode and content of class meetings.

I try to take such matters seriously. I do not believe teacher preparation is only for education majors who intend to teach beneath the college level; I try not to present teaching as more of a burden than an opportunity—although I am convinced that teaching does frequently interfere with research and writing, and that while my research does inform and benefit my teaching, the teaching of my undergraduate surveys does not benefit my research; and I am continually helping the students develop a dossier which outlines their teaching preparation and contains appraisals from myself and students.[9]

Outside the Classroom

Confining my remarks to the dissertation and teaching components of the graduate education at OSU is a bit misleading, for students surely need nurturing in many other skills if they are to survive. To this end, our faculty and students meet one evening each month, to discuss a potpourri of practical matters. Subjects which we have recently discussed include:

1. The politics of publishing: how to get manuscripts accepted by journals and publishers; which publishers want which kind of books and which journals want which kind of articles; how to revise an article to meet referees' objections; how to transform a dissertation into a book; the business of book reviewing.

2. The politics of grants and fellowships: what sorts of research projects are likely to attract funds; what type of preliminary work is necessary before applying for a grant; how to justify humanistic research for teachers/judges who may know little about the field; the most fatal omissions in ACLS/NEH/Woodrow Wilson applications; the importance of not "going it alone" when asking for money.

3. The politics of dress: virtually any combination of attire is accepted at most enlightened institutions, but some appearances are better than others, and not all institutions are enlightened.

In addition, before each session I usually recommend for the students' information, if not immediate reading, journal articles of importance. In modern Jewish history alone the number of journals publishing scholarly articles is well over two dozen, and this has been a time-saving procedure I believe.

The Peculiar Intimacy of Graduate Study

Finally, I wish to make a few comments on the private relationship between graduate professor and graduate student, a comradeship of extraordinary intensity. This relationship between professor and student is intimate in every sense of the word. Because they must work closely together, it is customary for student and adviser to spend a great deal of time in each other's company. At the very least, the individuals learn a great deal about each other, and it is surely not unusual for graduate professors to form long-lasting and very intense personal friendships with their students.[10]

The peculiar aspect of this relationship is that in it one party is completely sovereign, the other completely subservient—that is to say, the relationship is entirely undemocratic. The rules are generated by faculty, and they are promulgated, enforced, and adjudicated by that same faculty. It is perhaps analogous, at least in its initial stages, to the relationship between courtiers and nobles: contact must be made in the court and loyalty must be sworn; students woo their superiors, and sometimes the superiors offer blandishments to the students they want or need. Some matches, of course, are easy to make: when the proper professor meets the appropriate student, ceteris paribus, they make a match—the student is adopted as ward and swears fealty by saying, "I am a student of . . ."[11]

The student must concede that the professor is the appropriate party to provide the instruction, and concede that he/she is there to be "shaped" and that the professor will do much of the shaping. The student discovers what behaviors and accomplishments are expected—what values the professor holds dear and how to demonstrate respect for both mentor and discipline.

There are significant social/psychological, professional, intellectual, and material benefits for a graduate student in this close, academically oriented association with a respected professor, and probably foremost are the emotional rewards (heightened self-esteem, enhanced prestige, the fantasy of the eventual inheritance of power) one derives from studying with a mentor one admires and the help the mentor can give in identifying and securing jobs for the student.[12] On the other hand, often this kind of affiliation develops into a parent-child relationship with all the connected costs and benefits. Indeed, the dependency characteristic of a parent-child association is the most identifying psychological attribute of this relation, and Peter Lowenberg (History, UCLA) has enumerated the great costs of this dependency, especially if the professor does not feel equally attached or if the relationship is severed.[13]

The professor then seeks to make students as good as they can possibly become, and if that is not good enough, students often find themselves cast off. The better the student, the better the professor. Student and professor may generate and enact other private business, but anything external to the academic relationship can be evaluated only as it contributes to advancing or retarding the main relationship. It is not the purpose of graduate study to generate either love or friendship between student and professor, although both are possible concomitants.

The mentor has the responsibility to initiate the student into the lore and mysteries of the profession. Students learn about local (university) politics and national organization operations. They learn who should be respected, who opposed, and who ignored. They learn how judgments of scholarly quality are made. The fact is that the mentor controls, to a very large extent, what information and what values the student receives.

In order to justify the effort invested by the mentor in students, an exemplary accomplishment is required. The student who writes and publishes a paper, who wins an honor or fellowship, or who is awarded a post in an academic association testifies to the competency of the mentor. The latter's most important task, of course, is to help the advisee get a job in a favored department. By putting many good students into the professional world, professors advertise themselves and ensure themselves of a steady supply of students in the future.

It is hard to see the future of graduate study consisting of any relationship other than the one that now exists and that I have tried briefly to describe. To a large extent, graduate study is the last bastion of an ancient style of education where imitation of worthy masters was the keystone of learning. The student serves as an apprentice and learns the academic craft in the shadow of a more or less "benign" master. This is surely good—for the values of great teachers, their ideologies and their lives, ought to inspire and influence their pupils. Students do learn by emulation. The problem is that while most professors do not wish to produce carbon copies of themselves, many students would, apparently, like to be precisely that. We all know students, finished studying with masters, who have yet to become acquainted with the essential characteristics of their own mode of thinking. The danger is that many of us control rather than encourage independence of thought. I find, for example, that I can often observe and criticize my own ideas by listening to students mouth them ineptly.

The point is that in order to hear my own ideas less frequently from my students I have to accommodate myself to different personal styles, put up with annoying mannerisms, tolerate conflicting points of view, and learn to be patient with the student's fumbling efforts to learn. It has been a constant struggle to make certain that the increasing maturity of my students remains a more central concern than the gratification of my own or my students' infantile and neurotic needs and wishes. The very spirit of a graduate education is to help students to realize their own potentialities, to let them discover what they can really do, not as imitation or because it has been charted for them but because they have acquired a new view of themselves and their capacity.

But I find this challenge tough. All my students have ingrained in them by us teachers the assumption that the seat of knowledge is not in the learner. From elementary school through college they have been faced repeatedly with books written by "people who really know" and "teachers who know so much more." It has become relatively easy for them to acquire the belief that knowledge resides in books and in other people, not in themselves. This assumption is further fed in graduate school from experiences in regular course work where the emphasis is put on laying out conceptual structures. My mentor laid out so many and complex conceptual structures that I fought hard to retain the confidence that knowledge is not in these structures, not outside myself.

The task of the mentor is to guide students to the recognition that they are the seat of their knowing, that their own experience is to be taken as the basic authority for what they will say. But this is such a sharp psychological shift for my students that in fright and confusion, at least initially, they seek a way out. Efforts at escape take several forms: bold assertions of untried convictions; identification with an "authority" whose doctrines they accept and defend with more heat than light, and through whose mind they try to think; propensity for argument rather than open-ended discussion; meek and careful quotation of scholars in the field, taking great care never to express their own ideas except through the words of others; recurrent visitations to their adviser to seek assurance that what they are doing is "right." All these are techniques, however, to take the student away from self, and my task is to direct the research to bring them back to self, to lead students to begin sensing themselves as independent and worthy instruments of inquiry.[14]

Notes

1 See Mary Engle, "Thesis-Antithesis: Reflections on the Education of Researchers in Psychology," *American Psychologist* 21, no. 8 (August

1966): 781–87, and Laurence Veysey, *The Emergence of the American University* (Chicago, 1965), pp. 125–33.
2. Everett C. Ladd, Jr., and Seymour Martin Lipsett, "How Professors Spend Their Time: The 1975 Ladd-Lipsett Survey of U.S. Faculty Members," *Chronicle of Higher Education* 11, no. 5 (14 October 1975): 2.
3. See Bernard Berelson, *Graduate Education in the United States* (New York, 1960).
4. Louis D. Rubin, Jr., "What's Wrong with Graduate Literary Study?" *American Scholar* 32, no. 2 (Spring 1963): 222.
5. Robert Paul Wolff, as quoted in "For the Excellent Teacher: A Doctor of Arts Degree?" *Looking Ahead* 18, no. 5 (June 1970): 7.
6. Ann M. Heiss, "Graduate Education Today: An Instrument for Change?" *Journal of Higher Education* 39, no. 1 (January 1968): 1–10, and Heiss, *Challenge to Graduate Schools* (San Francisco, 1970).
7. For provocative insights on "personal and intellectual isolation," see Anne Robinson Taylor, "Becoming Observers and Specialists," in *Scholars in the Making: The Development of Graduate and Professional Students*, ed. Joseph Katz and Rodney T. Hartnett (Cambridge, Mass., 1976).
8. For the purpose of education and innovative ways of achieving them, one ought to closely examine Joseph J. Schwab, *College Curriculum and Student Protest* (Chicago, 1969).
9. Those concerned about inflicting graduate students, even good ones, on undergraduates, may wonder if there are any other sources of guinea pig students. There are; and quite frequently my students will offer courses through Continuing Education (community or extension courses) or in the institutions of the Jewish community.
10. For a description of the mentor relationship, see Daniel J. Levinson et al., "Periods in the Adult Development of Men: Ages 18–45," *Counseling Psychologist* 7, no. 1 (1976): 21–25.
11. Castiglione's paradigm of the courtier is discussed in Kenneth Burke, *A Rhetoric of Motives* (Berkeley, 1972), pp. 208–94.
12. Ann M. Heiss, "Berkeley Doctoral Students Appraise Their Academic Programs," *Educational Record* 48 (1967): 30–44.
13. Peter Lowenberg, in particular, talks about the possible frustration and anxiety that may result from this dependency in "Emotional Problems of Graduate Education," *Journal of Higher Education* 40 (1969): 610–23.
14. I have benefited from the critical comments of three friends: Professors Alan Avery-Peck, Tulane University; Michael Meyer, Hebrew Union College (Cincinnati); and Lewis Barth, Hebrew Union College (Los Angeles).

Part Three

Other Possibilities

10. The Three Academic Cultures of Graduate Education in Jewish Studies

Ivan G. Marcus

Graduate studies in Judaica take place in three major settings: American (and Canadian) universities, Israeli universities, and Jewish institutions of higher learning which grant the Ph.D. degree.[1] In substance and style a program located in any of these three types of institutions is shaped by a particular type of institutional culture. Despite the differences among the individual graduate institutions, each of the three constitute an academic culture with its own distinctive organizational setting and an appropriate theory of academic training. Each academic setting, in turn, influences how a graduate program in Jewish studies is conceptualized, and this affects the student's understanding of his or her career expectations. Viewed even more broadly, the three academic cultures are themselves reflections and refractions of the societies in which they are located. But this perspective would take us too far afield from my central concern which is the theoretical and practical frameworks of the three cultures of graduate Jewish education and scholarship today.

In most American universities, a student places an application to a department of a discipline or an area study, not to a department of Jewish studies. And although there is a recent trend at some universities toward the creation of semiautonomous programs or centers of Jewish studies, most graduate students are still expected to fulfill the requirements of a university department which is not concerned exclusively or primarily with Judaica. This means that the experience of most graduate students, regardless of their area within Jewish studies, is directed by the cultural norms of a disciplinary department. A student will think of him- or herself primarily as a historian, and then as a Jewish historian, or primarily as a student of religious studies, and only secondarily as a student of the history of Judaism. Framed within the department's expectations and requirements, the student's graduate school career and models of practicing scholar-teachers take on the same contours as the careers of others within that department who are not involved with an aspect of Jewish culture. Of necessity, all students will take a certain number of courses, language examinations, and seminars on theoretical and comparative matters which pertain to the discipline as a whole. The student of Jewish philosophy, for example, will structure a program around the discipline of philosophy shared by the faculty and other graduate students in that department and specialize within the department as others do. Moreover, in order to be able to speak a common language in term papers, examinations, qualifying or general examinations, the dissertation and defense, the student in an American university graduate program must learn to conceptualize what he or she does in Jewish studies in comparative terms so that others in the discipline can understand by analogy what is being said or written.

The emphasis in an American university departmental culture, then, on the theory and practice of a discipline and on comparative perspectives tends to make a graduate student in Jewish studies formulate what he or she does in broad terms in order to be intelligible to instructors and fellow students who have different interests and minimal or no frame of reference about Jewish studies. From the university's point of view, the end product of such training is a scholar who can write books and articles, write grant proposals, referee colleagues' work, and do a host of related academic tasks which flow from membership in the guild of the particular discipline.

To be sure, a departmental training within a discipline is exactly what a young scholar-teacher needs in order to be a successful American academician. For with a comparative and theoretical grounding in doctoral studies, the new Ph.D. is capable of functioning in an American university department which resembles the one in which the training took place. More than likely, he or she will be required to teach a share of general courses on method and theory or on traditions other than Jewish studies, and by being required to take such courses and absorb the ethos of the disciplinary training, the new instructor should be competent to provide this service to the department in addition to teaching and advising students in a particular research area of Jewish studies.

And yet, those who direct graduate programs in various areas of Jewish studies know that the advantages of the departmental system in training capable members of a disciplinary guild exist at the expense of something equally desirable in the training of a Jewish studies scholar: an in-depth knowledge of areas and periods of Jewish studies which lie outside the discipline one pursues in the departmental culture. Because a graduate student, for example, in Hebrew or Yiddish literature who studies in a comparative literature department is not expected to take courses outside of literature any more than a student of German or Romance literatures is, there is no departmental mandate for the student of Jewish literatures to study Hebrew Bible, Midrash, or modern Jewish history. And since most advisers in Jewish studies would agree that a student who wishes to understand Agnon ought to know these areas of Jewish studies anyway, the interconnectedness and cumulative character of Jewish culture being what they are, the student must study areas beyond the pale of the department's requirements for other students. Within the academic culture of the American university such in-depth knowledge not only is unavailable in at least some critical areas of study but is not a priority in principle from the department's viewpoint. Not that the university wants to create obstacles for the student of modern Hebrew fiction. Obviously, a student in general comparative literature should also know Bible and more than a little Greek and Latin literature and much more besides. But there is a limit to even the most demanding program, and in many cases the culture of the department does not promote the advanced study of fields of learning outside of the disciplinary framework.

Perhaps it is the tension between departmental norms and the broad range of extradisciplinary studies required for sound doctoral training in Jewish studies that has led to the relocation of some programs of Jewish studies from a particular disciplinary department to separate quarters with varying degrees of departmental affiliations. Clearly major needs are not being met in some disciplinary departments.

The tension between disciplinary training and the inner logic of

Jewish studies also surfaces after graduate school in the way one publishes one's research. By virtue of a departmental training in a discipline, the young scholar should submit manuscripts to the main journals of the discipline and think of other historians or philosophers or literary critics as his audience for published work. But the necessarily esoteric nature of much of advanced Jewish studies research, as far as most colleagues in one's discipline but not in Jewish studies are concerned, makes it more likely that technical research will get submitted to Jewish scholarly journals, and that only general, comparative, and theoretical translations and restatements of one's research will be successfully submitted to the prestige journals of the general discipline. This is not surprising because the establishment of American academe thinks in disciplinary terms and is totally unfamiliar with the subject matter of most areas of Jewish studies. The same tension applies to active membership of more than the most perfunctory nature in learned societies not connected with Jewish studies. The culture of the American university department is functional only to a certain degree, and beyond that it becomes dysfunctional.

If the American university departmental setting fosters a comparative perspective by viewing Jewish studies within the context of a discipline in the humanities, graduate programs in Israeli universities tend to be highly specialized and have departments of their own all under the umbrella of a Jewish studies center or institute. In a sense the picture is that of the American departmental setting turned on its head. Instead of being a small part of a general disciplinary department, the Israeli graduate student has a department of his own. For not only can an Israeli university afford to have a broad complement of scholars in several fields of Jewish studies, which most American universities cannot, but it also can locate them in various disciplinary departments of Jewish studies which are in, but not of, the rest of the faculty of the humanities. Graduate students work in the department of Jewish thought or the department of Jewish history which are structurally parallel to, but separate from, the department of philosophy or the department of history in the same university. This structure of specialization reflects an Israeli theory of higher Jewish education which, in a sense, is the polar opposite of that of the American disciplinary department.

This high degree of specialization at the graduate level is the top of an educational pyramid whose base is a broad elementary and secondary school education in several areas of Jewish studies as well as in areas of the humanities and sciences. An Israeli high school graduate is not only fluent in modern Hebrew, but also familiar with Hebrew Bible, some modern Hebrew literature, some Jewish history, and if he is from a religious school background, knows some classical rabbinics as well. Much of this knowledge may be rote memorization, but it is real and means that a firm foundation for some kind of Jewish studies exists from elementary school in subjects which many if not most American students must first acquire in college or graduate school.

As the Israeli student progresses after high school and the usual three-year stint in the army toward the B.A., specialization begins in earnest. The student takes no general liberal arts or science requirements but must immediately choose one or two majors for the three-year normal B.A. degree. The student who knows what he or she wants to pursue for an eventual M.A. and Ph.D. in Jewish studies can begin at once majoring in one or two departments of Jewish studies. Beyond that, the M.A. requires further concentration in one department which, in turn, leads to the doctoral dissertation.

Although the Israeli doctoral student has accumulated a vast amount of information from earlier years of schooling in Jewish subjects, there is no mandate in graduate school to study at an advanced level in any department outside the one of one's doctoral specialization or to work in the non-Jewish-studies parallel department in the same discipline. Thus the level of learning of an Israeli doctoral student in almost all areas outside of a relatively narrow field within Jewish studies is likely to be a secondary school one.

Throughout the demanding M.A., which is closer to an American M. Phil. than to the almost perfunctory American M.A., a student in Jewish history, for example, may never take a course in methodology, historiography, or in the philosophy of history in the general department of history. Comparative and theoretical issues which are so central to the American university disciplinary departmental culture are not important in Israel. Instead, the M.A. student takes a specific number of courses in one department of Jewish studies. The degree follows the successful completion of a series of courses, examinations, and papers all within the same departmental context.

To an American university student, whose culture is comparative in emphasis and oriented theoretically, the Israeli graduate student's culture seems to be severely limiting. This impression is further reinforced by the absence in doctoral studies of any foreign language requirements apart from English which is usually begun some time in elementary school. Some of the most accomplished doctoral students and scholars do not have the ability or confidence or interest to publish or lecture in any language other than Hebrew. Of course, many, if not most, American graduate students and scholars in Jewish studies have some difficulty lecturing and writing in fluent Israeli academic Hebrew, but the difference in the size of the audiences of each language outside of Israel makes the comparison almost meaningless.

Yet, within an Israeli context, the specialized Hebrew culture of such a doctorate is entirely functional. Since most Ph.D. graduates are likely to teach and write in their own subfield in an Israeli secondary school, teachers college, or university department of the same specialization, there is little reason to change the emphasis in their training for the degree. Ample opportunities exist to publish, teach, and lecture in Hebrew. Even American journals of Jewish studies allow Israeli scholars to publish in Hebrew or to submit manuscripts in Hebrew for translation into English. But most Israeli scholars do not submit manuscripts in English to general journals in disciplinary areas related to their field of Jewish studies, and many cannot teach abroad except in institutions which enable them to function in the style which is familiar to them at home. Unquestionably the academic cultures in American and Israeli universities reflect the two societies in which they exist.

A third setting for Jewish graduate education is in Jewish institutions of higher learning in America. Although thus far I have dealt in general ways with American and Israeli programs, I want to illustrate the third academic cultural setting with one example, the Jewish Theological Seminary of America's graduate school. I shift the focus from the genus to the species not only because I know my own institution better than any of the others in this small group but also because I think that the differences among the Jewish institutions are greater than those which obtain within the other two categories. Because it is harder to generalize in a valid way about the Seminary, Yeshiva University, Hebrew Union College, and Dropsie, I prefer to outline in some depth the program I know well rather than review each of the four superficially

In some ways, the Seminary's graduate school was reorganized in the late 1960s in light of the growth of university teaching opportunities in this country and Canada. In other ways, it builds on decades of academic traditions of learning inherited from Eastern European Jewish religious institutions and on Western European universities as well as on American academic influences. Possibly because Israeli university programs were also influenced by many of the same European educational traditions, the Seminary doctoral program shares some of the features found there as well as others which derive from American university culture. Thus if the American and Israeli university are two distinctive and polar cultures for Jewish studies, the Seminary setting is a third which combines elements from both while also being a unique expression of its own values about learning.

Whereas the American university places great stress in doctoral training on a comparative, humanistic framework within a discipline, and the Israeli programs emphasize depth in textual and philological methodologies and erudition within a highly specialized field of Jewish studies, the Seminary's conception of graduate education includes both of these and adds a third. It also requires students to study several fields and areas of Jewish studies at the M.A. level before specialization in one field.

As in American university programs, students in the Seminary's graduate school take a disciplinary or area approach which is institutionalized in course work, foreign language requirements (Hebrew, French, German, plus additional languages as needed), comprehensive oral examinations, and an oral defense of dissertation. In addition to this emphasis on a discipline within the Jewish studies major area of concentration, however, all students are affiliated by means of a specially worked out consortium with a parallel disciplinary department at a university where a minor is taken in the related general discipline. One or more faculty advisers at that university department are available to the Seminary doctoral student in course work, orals, and dissertation writing.

To be sure, because the student is at the Seminary and not a university, most of his or her time will not be spent in a general disciplinary department in which Jewish studies is only a minor part of the department's concern. Of necessity, there will be less emphasis on translating what one does into an idiom which those not in Jewish studies can understand. This skill must be acquired at the university in connection with the minor, but the student also has to work at this in relation to the major area of concentration. The culture of the Seminary's program does not promote this any more than the culture of the American university department fosters the broad study of several cognate areas of Jewish studies outside of the discipline.

Although the Seminary's graduate school, like the Israeli university programs, is divided into specialized departments, all in Jewish studies, the Seminary program requires all graduate students pursuing the doctorate to achieve a degree of proficiency in all major areas of Jewish studies equivalent to the M.A. level. The requirement that students take a significant sequence of courses in Hebrew Bible, rabbinic literature, Jewish history, philosophies of Judaism, and Jewish literature in which they read texts and secondary readings in Hebrew is not a realistic expectation in most American university programs, which rarely have the faculty depth to meet such a requirement. More important, such a requirement reflects a theoretical posture toward Jewish studies which the Seminary advocates and which is not in keeping with the disciplinary orientation of American university departments in which Jewish studies are located. The Seminary's program expresses a belief that Jewish culture is a complex, interrelated whole and that a scholar trained in one area ought to be familiar with and skilled in several areas including the classics of Jewish studies: Hebrew Bible and rabbinics.

The Seminary Ph.D. program's combination of a consortial affiliation with a general university department in a discipline, on the one hand, and an M.A.-level distribution requirement in five areas of Jewish studies in addition to intensive Hebrew language proficiency, on the other, makes it both comparative and humanistic as well as broadly grounded in Jewish studies without sacrificing the central culminating stage of a focus in one field of Jewish studies in one discipline.

Like the American and Israeli university programs, the Seminary's doctoral training reflects an underlying theory about the character of Jewish studies and expresses the values of a specific academic culture. The decades-old tradition of philological humanistic scholarship has increasingly been complemented by a process of Americanization, the result being that a student who receives a Ph.D. from the graduate school should be able to participate fully in the academic culture of the discipline in which he or she works and in Israeli and American university Jewish studies circles. This model of the doctorate in Jewish studies represents a new direction for the Seminary which used to think of itself as the primary employer of its graduating doctoral candidates. Prior to the proliferation of college Jewish studies programs, the Seminary and other Jewish institutions of higher learning were the primary market for new Ph.D.'s in the field. The reorganized graduate program is an attempt to come to terms with the realities of American academic life in Jewish studies. The question remaining, however, is whether the ideological interests of an institution like the Seminary are at odds with the academic agenda of a graduate school in Jewish studies.

Since the Seminary was founded and continues to be a rabbinical school and a cantorial school in addition to being an undergraduate college and a graduate school, it is often questioned how genuinely academic and disinterested the nonrabbinical graduate programs are in view of the denominational context of the institution as a whole. The issue of an institution's values and biases is usually raised about the Jewish religious institutions and occasionally about Israeli universities but rarely about American university programs. It is worth considering this important matter a little more closely. If we focus on the ideal direction and character of each type of institutional culture, it seems to be the case that values are operating in all three. That is what is meant by a "culture": there is an ethos, a set of values which is supposed to direct action, and a set of assumptions about the way things are, a world view.

The truth is that specific values are at work in Israeli universities and American universities as well as at Jewish religious institutions. In Israeli doctoral programs there are historical and cultural assumptions about Jewish civilization, its central relationship to the Land of Israel, and an affirmation of an entity referred to as "the Jewish People." American university training also is shaped by certain assumptions and biases of different kinds. Although the dominant ethos of the university promotes disinterested research and teaching, which can only benefit Jewish studies, the stress on comparability and on theories which are supposed to apply universally to all examples may not fit Judaism. This is not because Judaism is incomprehensible but because some of the theories are derived from Christian or Marxist or Freudian models which are dissonant with Jewish culture. Even more problematic today is latent or manifest hostility toward Jewish studies generated by contemporary political issues, such as the Arab-Israeli conflict, or by Christian theological postures thinly veiled in an academic veneer.

Despite the possibility that each of the three academic cultures is susceptible to the criticism of holding back academic progress because of particular types of biases, it is often taken for granted that only in Jewish religious institutions are academic activities and doctoral training and scholarship necessarily compromised by the religious ideology and orientation of the institution. The historical and psychological reasons why this perception exists need not concern us here. What is of interest is that such a conflict is presumed to exist in a Jewish religious institution and is presumed not to exist in an American university.

In reality, each graduate student and scholar, regardless of his or her academic setting, must struggle with questions of personal identity as well as with the "cult of relevance," be it to an American, Israeli, or specific American religious audience. What does set a Jewish religious institution apart from the other two cultures is not so much that in it academic research is inevitably colored by religious enthusiasm, as that its priorities about its responsibility toward its religious constituency and the outside scholarly world are different. Unlike a university whose primary purpose is to promote research and train and educate students, an institution like the Seminary has a different primary purpose: to provide leadership for the religious movement of Conservative Judaism. There will of necessity be a balancing of this goal with the academic goals which are a university's raison d'être. The existence of this tension, however, does not preclude the possibility that both activities can take place and that graduate students and faculty can be members of the worldwide academic community in their field in Jewish studies.

One consequence of the existence of three academic cultures of graduate education in Jewish studies is the fact that in all three cases the scholar-teacher who is a member of one academic culture is marginal, in some sense, to the others. For example, even after completing an American university training program, in which a disciplinary focus provides the dominant set of norms and loyalties, a graduate in Jewish studies may be reluctant to view journals and associations of the discipline as the major outlet for professional advancement and tend instead to rely on Jewish equivalents. The American-trained scholar will also not have much of a shared universe of discourse with an Israeli colleague who did not receive significant training in America. Instead of focusing primarily on texts and their reliability—good philological concerns—an American scholar will also be oriented toward critical questions and methodologies which are disciplinary concerns and unintelligible to most Israeli scholars. In some fields, students and scholars in American and Israeli universities may be so marginal to each other that they may talk past one another or simply ignore those not living in the same academic cultural world.

Although opportunities for exchange between members of the two most distinctive cultures in Jewish studies, the American and Israeli university programs, do occur in visiting pre- and postdoctoral programs, all too often one's psychosocial mind-set is confirmed rather than disturbed by the experience, since one is preconditioned to see some things and not to see and assimilate others.

A different but equally poignant kind of marginality can affect a Seminary-trained doctoral student who has benefited from the reorganized doctoral program of the past decade. In some ways he or she gains some of the advantages of the other two cultures but is also marginal to both. For example, a student trained at the Seminary may have some doubt as to how thorough his or her grounding is in the general disciplinary field which the student pursues as a minor, not in a matriculated degree program at a university.

In addition, a doctoral student who is required, as at the Seminary, to work toward an M.A.-level of proficiency in several areas of Jewish studies, in addition to concentrating in one field and discipline for the doctorate, may feel some estrangement from an Israeli colleague whose nonspecialty Jewish studies may be quantitatively formidable, if selective, but who may not have studied any of them beyond secondary school. An additional factor which can separate Seminary from Israeli students is the American academic experience which the former bring to his or her Seminary doctoral studies. Since an American B.A. is significantly different from an Israeli degree, the values gained in acquiring each will continue to color later graduate training.

The result of the existence of these three academic cultures is a growing polarization in the field of Jewish studies as a whole. In addition to ideological or religious motivations, which may lead a potential doctoral student to study at an Israeli university or at a Jewish religious institution, it appears that the cultures of these two settings promote marginality to the culture of the American university setting for Jewish studies, and vice versa. If we do not want to accept three cultures in Jewish studies, something needs to be done to bring some coherence to the field. The exchange of individual students and faculty can do only so much to bridge these cultural chasms. In addition, a new forum is needed, such as an institute for advanced Jewish studies which is not affiliated with, or dominated by, any one degree-granting institution. Such an institute should be located in America and be modeled on other independent research institutes in America and Europe. It would complement existing research institutes of Jewish studies and define as one of its goals an ongoing discussion of the three academic cultures in Jewish studies today. An awareness of legitimately differing approaches and values applied to the study of the same historical culture could illuminate everyone's work and provide a unifying focus for the field as a whole. By better understanding each other's academic culture, we may better appreciate our own. But first we need to face openly the implications of the three academic cultures which presently exist for the training of doctoral students in Jewish studies.

Note

1 For thoughts about Jewish studies at an American university and at an Israeli university, see my "Bringing Judaica to the Liberal Arts," *Yale Alumni Magazine,* November, 1981, pp. 25–28, and "Last Year in Jerusalem," *Response* 44 (Spring 1983).

Part Four

The Larger Context

11. Jewish Studies and the New Humanities

Jacob Neusner

When the study of the Jews and Judaism entered universities, the subject came as part of what we now realize formed a new wave of humanistic learning. The new humanities comprised subjects never before studied—histories, literatures, philosophies, religions, human experiences, and insights formerly neglected. What happened in the 1960s and early 1970s turned out to be a considerable expansion in the established curriculum of humanistic learning in American and Canadian universities. Departments of history, formerly centered upon American and Western European history, made a place for regions and groups formerly ignored, such as Asia, on the one side, and blacks and Jews on the other. Programs and departments of literature, formerly interested in English, American, French, German, and Russian literature, began to ask students to read Afro-American and Latin American writings. The single most dramatic development of the 1960s proved to be the opening of the study of religion to encompass traditions and religious communities beyond Christianity, first and foremost, Judaism. In these and other ways, therefore, the humanistic disciplines paid attention to history, literature, and religion of groups formerly assumed to have none worth studying.

If we ask ourselves why, at just that time, university humanists discovered importance in subjects formerly not recognized at all, we may point to three factors.

First, in the 1950s, America had assumed a considerable position in world affairs, with the result that Americans took an interest in parts of the world formerly beyond the horizon. Accordingly, Russian studies were born, and alongside, the conception of area studies took shape. An area or region such as the Soviet Union, or the Near and Middle East, or North Africa, might provide the focus for diverse disciplines and their practitioners: historians, literary specialists, not to mention anthropologists, geographers, sociologists, political scientists, scholars of religions. Once the stranglehold of the established areas and regions—Western Europe mainly, America secondarily—gave way, area studies would encompass the whole of human civilization. Indeed, the first important break with convention lay in the establishment of American studies as a recognized field of not only literature and history, but everything else. Now once the universities had made a place for regional studies, it would be difficult to include one region and yet exclude some other.

The reason for the difficulty, second, lay in the entry, into the classes of those whose opinions counted, of formerly submerged or ignored groups. Whether constituted as a group by race, ethnic origin, religion, or gender, these groups wished to make their presence felt in higher education. Most could not state exactly what that ought to mean. But they knew they did not wish any longer to be ignored, treated as invisible. Who were they? Jews and Catholics, then blacks, Puerto Ricans and "other Hispanics," Asian-Americans, American Indians, not to mention Scandinavians, Italians and Poles, and women—the list is long and varied. The components of the list do not compare to one another, except in the shared aspiration to enter the academic curriculum. As I said, no one could say for sure what that entry ought to mean. But with the enormous diversification of the constituency of universities, with Jews no longer carefully counted one by one and instructed not to count at all, with blacks no longer completely isolated, with other groups no longer forgotten, with women no longer merely tolerated so long as they acted as men wanted them to, universities clearly had to change. They had to come abreast of fundamental changes already taking place in the character of American society and culture. Social change produces symbol change. The curriculum of a university, whatever else it does, serves as an enormously effective symbolic statement about what matters and what does not.

So with the emergence of America as a world power with global interests and with the glacial shifting of the structure of American

Jewish Studies and the New Humanities 169

society to provide a final accommodation for the new immigrants' children of two and three generations earlier (including the black immigrants from farm to city and South to North), the demand for the end to exclusion in society carried echoes even into the campus of the university. These two factors—a change in the nation's politics, a shift in the nation's catalogue of recognized groups—joined with yet a third to produce the changes I have characterized as the birth of the new humanities.

That third change affected the universities alone. It consisted in the effects of the tidal wave of growth, as the generation of the postwar baby boom reached university age, on the one side, and as the proportion of college-age young people choosing to go on for higher education vastly increased, on the other. These two facts joined to impose an enormous increase in size upon old universities and to force the creation of new universities, colleges, community colleges, and the like. What followed in the age of unprecedented expansion, including inclusion, in the college population, of groups formerly excluded from it, could have surprised no one. New teachers had to be hired. These teachers could no longer come only from the protected castes—"Anglo-Saxons" and those who acted like them. So just as women demanded a place and attention in the curriculum, so some women found a place, also, in faculties, as did Jews in numbers unthinkable a generation earlier, Catholics, once no more welcome than Jews, and pretty much anybody who could present appropriate credentials. The homogeneity of old American universities, with their old American faculties and their old American names and genealogies, gave way. A small indicator of the shift derives from the development of professing Jewish communities in college towns in which, formerly, Jews served as a curiosity at best. As one of the first Jews to reach tenure at Dartmouth College, I remember what things were like, how much change I brought in my very conviction that, at sundown on Friday, something changed in Hanover, so far as I was concerned.

Once universities had opened their doors to the much larger and more diverse social and ethnic constituencies than they had ever known, the question confronted faculties and students alike: what do we do now? The answer lay in the decision to do more than had been done before. That meant that students would seek to study what was familiar in their own background. But this was quite natural and just as students had always done. The old Americans had always known what was theirs—classics, after all, was a gentleman's hobby, English literature belonged to the descendants of English immigrants, and American history was the history written by the old Americans' great-grandfathers. A certain snobbery, of course, protected these scheduled subjects; people absorbed the prejudice that, quite naturally and predictably, these were things *any* educated person should know. Knowing these things, this list of selected books (the one hundred books for the one hundred families that count)—that knowledge defined education. Hence a core curriculum and general education seemed possible. No one needed to ask about the excluded hundreds of thousands of books, classic to the excluded groups, and the millions of excluded families, out of which students now came. Everybody knew what was what: what was of worth and represented taste, what shaped thoughts worth thinking, what defined values worth adopting. And, it should be added, people who knew these worthwhile things also could look forward to careers of worth and standing: in banks, law firms, corporate offices, hospitals and universities, and the other protected professions reserved for those who knew the scheduled subjects and came from the right castes.

All that had to change, and it has changed. But no one has yet reckoned with how to take hold of the change and make sense of it. For the change proved not entirely for the good. True, the old humanities may have insisted upon classics and biblical Hebrew, but not Italian and never modern Hebrew; American and Western European history, but not Latin American, Canadian, or Eastern European history, let alone Asia, let alone Africa, let alone Polynesia, which have no histories (an opinion I myself took for granted as a youth); American and British literature, but not Afro-American literature and not Polish or French-Canadian. But the old humanities preserved not only privilege but also a center, a sense of purpose. Their imperial view did encompass everybody. That is the main point. The old humanities indeed imagined that they had something to say to the whole of humanity and that what they had to say demanded a universal audience. The established humanities could indeed point to books they believed everyone should read. And they could say why.

The same reasons pointed to traits of intellectual excellence and relevance. They therefore could imagine such a thing as a general education. So, they held, people could determine why one book did matter more than another, and why one philosophical tradition deserved close and careful scrutiny, while another preserved mere gibberish. The power of the conventional and established humanities lay in the exercise of educated taste and reasoned judgment. The promise of the old humanities to impose order upon the chaos of information, to sort things out and to select some few that truly changed persons and nurtured character and culture—that promise has never met competition from the motley crowd of new humanities now demanding entry to the campus, giving only politics as the reason.

For what did the new humanities offer to justify their entry into the realm of the disciplined intellect? The mere presence of a new sort of human being, formerly excluded, hardly constituted a persuasive argument. After all, that new person, whether black, Catholic, woman, or Jew, could readily enter the classics of the established curriculum and adopt its values. Generations of "minorities" had done so. But what universally accessible human experience did the new constituencies bring to the campus, to measure up to the classics of human intellect that, all together, had constituted the old humanities? Where was the Jewish Aquinas or Plato, the black Shakespeare, the Catholic equivalent to the Reformation that everyone studies with such admiration? And, when the new humanities pointed to their heritage of art, music, fiction, and poetry, few were prepared to take a look. So people took for granted, both old and new alike, that the blacks would come, to be sure. But then blacks would study what blacks had done. Jews would study Jewish studies. Women would study women's studies. But everyone, anyhow, would still study the familiar philosophy, the Shakespeare, the Reformation that everyone had always studied, in the ways in which everyone had always studied them.

So was formed the benign consensus of the 1970s: insiders teaching private things to insiders, and everyone learning public things as they had always been taught. Everyone for a time accepted the compromise. The newcomers felt quite at home, as well they should, having never left their ghettoes. The established humanities retained their ultimate governance. Making room for newcomers, they found themselves essentially unchanged. The old privileges endured and did not even have to be shared. What emerged, then, through the 1970s, was curricular tokenism, a kind of intellectual affirmative action: the black women receptionists, the clever Jews in the research department, to be sure—but the board of directors would come from the same good folk that had supplied members for generations past. Everyone would be contented.

Unhappily, the easy compromise of the 1970s has fallen away. The new humanities cannot sustain themselves within its terms. The established humanities turn out to be unable to explain themselves any longer. The newcomers prove inadequate to the labor, and the old-timers have fallen into bankruptcy. How so?

The new humanities, in their dominant form, lay no important claim upon the university. They consist of Jews teaching Jewish things to Jews, and blacks to blacks, and women to women, as I said. But universities understand themselves as places where everybody speaks to whom it may concern. Scholars speak about truth and matters of scholarship and interpretation. None sustains private truth and speaks of inaccessible experience and demands assent to unreasoned interpretation. Accordingly, the established distinction between insider and outsider, upon which the new humanities have built, finds no solid ground in the foundations of universities.

The new humanities, moreover, lay no claim to have much to say to the community at large. So they offer no reasoned counter to the argument that some things do matter more than others, white things more than black, Aquinas more than Maimonides, the Old Testament as Protestants read it more than scripture and tradition as Catholics know them or "the whole Torah of Moses, our rabbi," as Jews revere it. Once the new humanities conceded that theirs was an essentially private and particular heritage, to be promoted for paraochial purposes (to give blacks self-confidence, to persuade Jews to remain Jewish), they also turned themselves into mere pressure groups on the campus, extensions of political forces deriving from outside the campus.

The result for black studies has proved disastrous. The *Washington Post* reports, in an article by James Lardner (December 3, 1982), that in the late sixties and early seventies, there were more than five hundred formal programs in black or Afro-American studies. Today only 275 programs survive; of these, only 65 or 70 are departments. Scholars of black studies concede that their field has entered "a state of near-crisis." Why? Because the black students themselves avoid black studies. The scholars excuse themselves by explaining that the students are "more job-conscious and more interested in courses that will make them employable." This is pure self-indulgence. In this same period classics has enjoyed a renaissance, although few jobs these days demand knowledge of Attic Greek or the ability to read Plato in the original. Lest the *Washington Post* report be regarded as exceptional, I point also to Edward B. Fiske's article in the *New York Times,* January 13, 1983. He too reports that, in black studies, enrollments decline, and while people once estimated there were as many as eight hundred black studies programs, today estimates fall in the range of about five hundred. Enrollments exhibit a decline of approximately 25 percent from the highs of a decade ago. Anyone who doubts that the same story may be told of Jewish studies and other ethnic studies needs only to attend a meeting of the learned societies of those fields. The atmosphere in times past provided more evidence of hope and energy.

Not only the newer subjects in the humanities, but also newer disciplinary foci give evidence of regression. The new field of the academic study of religion, which was born in the later 1940s and fully realized in the 1960s as part of the larger development under discussion here, grows old and feeble. At its national meeting just now the scholars held a caucus of "endangered departments." One participant guessed, "Every religion department from Springfield, Missouri, to the tip of Maine is endangered, whether the department chairmen know it or not." The simple fact is that people take for granted you can have a university without black, Jewish, women's, or religious studies, but you cannot have a university without history, English, philosophy, or sociology.

What went wrong? The new humanities have not yet taken the measure of universities. Universities have not yet imparted their distinctive character to the new humanities. That is one fact, with two complementary effects. The new humanities have a future in universities only if they will join the sort of discourse that universities nurture. The university, for its part, must build its future upon the broadest social foundations and draw upon the deepest cultural resources of human experience and culture. And that can happen only when the university demonstrates, as it has not yet shown, the universal power of its program of inquiry to illuminate the analysis of human experience across the globe, to make interesting and public what is presently self-serving and private. So each side, whether the new or the old, the outsider or the one at home, bears part of the responsibility for the reform of the new humanities, and, with that reform, the renaissance of the academic humanities as we now know them.

At issue in universities always and everywhere is only one thing: scholarship. By scholarship I mean systematic learning of important things, the conduct of experiments to test theories, the pursuit of possibilities of knowledge—in sum, the game and play of unending learning, purposeful curiosity, pointed and skeptical argument about what we think we know. What matters in the end, what decides which universities make a difference and which do not, is solely scholarship.

In universities, to be sure, frail humanity works on lesser things. Wars are fought for trivialities such as this one's good name and that one's right to work or self-respect. But however things appear to the ones who invest their energies in politics, in the end truth, meaning scholarship, settles all substantial questions. The difference between universities and other large institutions is that in universities in the end you do not build a career on the blood of someone else. You cannot achieve lasting importance through politics, even through popularity, but only through intellectual achievement. That is the stern fact of life, the unyielding law of institutions of learning.

Scholarship by its nature pays no attention to claims of privacy. A proposition that one cannot understand unless qualified by gifts of genealogy or other-than-intellectual standing gains no hearing at all. A course on a subject only Jews can understand will not endure and in the end will attract no Jews. A book that speaks to people only if to begin with they believe the book to be true or self-evidently important will enjoy a long life on the library shelf. Such a book is a mere curiosity, something for anthropology to interpret, not for the humanities to confront. Such a course serves no relevant purpose. In

Jewish Studies and the New Humanities

the end, even those amenable to special pleading will turn away. For, as I said, at issue in universities is scholarship alone. Scholarship, as we know it, comes to us from the age of reason and speaks to us of what is subject to public scrutiny and reasonable judgment. That is not to argue that a book for a handful of believers will never find its readers beyond those believers, or that a course directed to a preselected audience will never reach outsiders. It is rather my view that such books, such courses, in the end go the way of all claims at reaching judgments through other than critical and reasonable modes of thought. They enjoy the fate of all truths that claim to be known a priori, and not through inductive inquiry and testing, all convictions about a knowledge of reality exempt from processes of verification and falsification—the oblivion of all deductive propositions. Scholarship as we practice it is inductive, aims at falsifying or verifying all claims to truth, subjects all propositions to the same critical and reasonable modes of thought.

We organize culture and preserve learning in more than a single way, that is, through more kinds of institutions than one. Universities constitute only one sort of institution of learning. In addition, for Judaism, to *yeshivot,* there are, after all, museums. They are staffed by expert curators. Museums also preserve knowledge. Curators also know a great deal. The difference between a university and a museum, between a professor and a curator, lies in how facts are displayed. In a museum people lay things out, they show the artifacts of culture, the glyphs and tablets that preserve it. The curator proves expert on the details of a given culture. His highest form of learning is ethnography, the accurate description of a well-preserved culture, the reliable portrayal of what a social group has made to express and preserve its viewpoint. A museum may accommodate what a group deems private and serves to preserve what people claim to be unable to communicate. That is the power of a museum, the gift of the curator, the contribution of ethnography.

When professors serve as curators, scholarship falls into one of two inappropriate categories. Scholars either return to that level of culture we know as hunting and gathering. Or they engage in the game of show-and-tell. Or they do both. They may achieve stunningly expert knowledge of details, lovingly and expertly hunted down and gathered. They then present what they have collected in the secure knowledge that others implicitly concede the self-evident importance of the collection. So scholarship becomes no more than one of its essential components: ethnography alone. Then the professor serves as a curator, the university as a museum, and all the different subjects of the humanities fall into place, each one in its room, all of them in their carefully arranged showcases.

What is right with all this is simple: without ethnography, there can be no anthropology. So too without the work of hunting and gathering, showing and telling, there can be no substance to the humanities. What is wrong is equally self-evident to me: the work in the end proves mindless because no one wants to make any points. No one argues any propositions relevant to anyone outside the showcase room. When universities treated ethnic studies as special, when practitioners of those studies claimed to speak only to their own kind, then scholarship fell away. So far as the new humanities were to flourish, it would be through stupefying learning about what no one much cared to know. Playing an endless game of show and tell, justified by self-indulgent special pleading, the professors of the new humanities hunted and gathered everything but a reason for their profession. For their part, the universities accommodated what in fact most people despised and would dismiss as soon as they decently could. For universities are not museums, and professors mean to add to knowledge, not only preserve and display it.

Since universities draw nurture from the societies that sponsor them and the politics that give effect to social policy, universities will hardly benefit from reversion to the old world of institutionalized prejudice and cultural snobbery. American society will never tolerate the reintroduction of quotas to exclude Jews, let alone the implementation of the bigotry that blacks cannot learn and women should not. For their part, the new humanities fail the universities and the society that depends upon them, if they continue the exclusionary theory of themselves. The task of the new humanities is to gain legitimate entry into the intellectual life of the universities. The task of the universities is to insist upon the same principles of reasoned discourse and public accounting of all propositions that have framed scholarship and defined learning we deem worthwhile. Both parties have to move from the initial stage of an uneasy accommodation of the old to the new, the reticence of the new to gain true entry into the old. How shall we frame matters so that universities may gain the strength of the great creative forces of our day, represented as they are by new groups coming of age, new bodies of learning demanding analysis, new sorts of human experience requiring interpretation?

Let me frame the answer in terms of the curriculum. How shall we achieve the integration of the new humanities within the university's conception of its own work? To begin with, let me state my own philosophy: *I teach students*. By the way, what I teach to students is about Judaism—in that order. To generalize, we teach two things: (1) a subject to (2) a student. What we teach students, through any subject, is about thinking, about using their minds for specific tasks. The curriculum then consists of two components: first, information we offer, which students learn, and, second, our example of how we compose that information into intelligible propositions, arguments about possibilities, which students may choose to imitate and improve. Whether we teach undergraduates or graduate students, the issue is the same. Students should be concerned with modes of analysis and means of interpretation, through which they learn the particulars of information. When we impart information without articulating how we have formulated matters and worked them out in one way rather than some other, we do only part of our work, the part, alas, most rapidly forgotten or rendered obsolete. In the phrasing of my co-worker, William Scott Green, University of Rochester, "Teaching means to teach students how to do something, how to know something, how to understand something."

By this criterion, one subject serves as well as any other, the history of the Jews as much as the history of the ancient Romans or the medieval French or the modern Americans, the literature of the American blacks as much as the literature of the English, the religious world of Islam as much as that of Christianity, the Roman Catholic experience of Christianity as much as the Protestant—not to exclude the woman's view of things as much as the man's. For whatever we teach stands or falls by the same criterion: does the subject at hand present the possibility of analyzing generally intelligible propositions? Does the area of learning generate theses worth sustained testing, ideas capable of providing insight beyond themselves and transcending the limits of the world that gave them first light? To accord to white male experience the status of the norm and black or female experience the status of the abnormal then no longer proves a proposition worth attention. For human experience properly described, analyzed, and interpreted speaks to us all. But without analysis and argument, no experience *self-evidently* establishes the norm (or diverges from it).

Accordingly, universities engaged in scholarship not only accommodate the new humanities. They no longer can imagine scholarship in ignorance of the corpus of human experience and achievement taken up in those new humanities. Rigorous thought about what matters by definition focuses then upon black as much as white, just as biology or anthropology, respectively, inquires into the blood of anyone or the social culture of any group. The very nature of the disciplines and discourse of university scholarship requires the full recognition of the new humanities alongside the established ones. Why? Because we cannot do our work without them all.

What must come to an end, however, has also to be specified. Let me express the matter in terms of Jewish studies. Jewish studies locate themselves in universities. But they have yet to become part of universities. They remain an area of learning in which the bulk of the practitioners see themselves as part of a world outside of universities: intruders. In that other world, the familiar realm of Jewish learning practiced by Jews for Jews, Jewish learning regards itself as self-evidently important and valid. The questions it raises—questions of fact, questions of interpretation—emerge from the Jewish experience treated in isolation from the experience of the rest of humanity. Those questions are urgent because Jews need the answers. The way in which one finds the answers gains definition from established modes and procedures of Jewish learning in particular. These turn out to be conducted essentially beyond the accounting to a broader range of learning and in behalf of an essentially private constituency.

So Jews write books for Jews about Jews and imagine no broader public. Scholarship deemed in this context to be great proves erudite and technical, self-absorbed and narrow, limited and parochial. We admire the erudition; we must master the technicalities. We in universities, however, remove ourselves from our life when we accept the limitation, the parochiality, above all the self-absorption. The principal problem derives from the failure to treat problems or answer questions. Jewish learning under Jewish auspices provides information. It rarely makes the effort to relate that information to something beyond itself. When scholarship is at issue, then textbooks emerge that espouse a viewpoint, find organization within a theory, propose to answer a question or solve a problem. But textbooks for Jewish studies in general disgorge information. Scholarship yields a curriculum, a systematic program of orderly learning, through which students learn how to do first one thing, then the next. Just as the field of religious studies has yet to develop a curriculum, because it lacks a program of study, so the field of Jewish studies yields nothing one might call systematic organization of the subject (except for instruction in elementary Hebrew). A field with no agenda, (in William Green's phrase) no cognitive purpose, no disciplined curiosity also nurtures no curriculum. Without a limited program of inquiry, without generally understood (if not universally accepted) standards by which we can tell a bad piece of work from a good one, without a reasoned problematic and a curiosity subject to explanation and transmission, Jewish studies also generate no energy. So we find the source of the lethargy. That is why arguments about why Jewish students are dutybound to take courses in Jewish studies today circulate as a rationale for the field. It is the usual appeal to guilt. And that explains also the intellectual lethargy and academic bankruptcy of the Association for Jewish Studies, the American Academy of Jewish Research, and the other academic learned societies that claim to embody Jewish studies in meetings from year to year and in journals lacking all cogency.

When scholarship is at issue, then we can point to how a field is to be introduced. When people trained in Jewish studies for the doctorate enter disciplinary departments or disciplinary fields, as they commonly do, they discover an interesting problem. If they join history departments, they find themselves unable to participate in the introduction to Western civilization. When they join philosophy departments, they find it difficult to teach the introduction to philosophy. When they enter departments of religious studies, a fair number of them will face the task of offering the introduction to religion, whether formulated as "methods in the study of religions" or "theories of religion" or the principal religious traditions of the West. This they cannot do. Few of the more influential and admired figures in Jewish studies, for example, the heroes of the young people who make up the bulk of the participants at such ethnocentric celebrations as Association for Jewish Studies meetings, could give the introductory course in the departments of which they are members, excluding only Hebrew. If, further, they find employment in departments of Jewish studies, few of these same widely appreciated heroic figures could even define what such an introductory course in such a department ought to teach.

How shall we proceed? In my view the task falls upon the shoulders of the new humanities. If we claim right of entry, ours is the burden of presenting a valid ticket of admission. No one doubts that we belong. The books people wrote in the submerged and ignored sectors of humanity, those of the wrong religion, race, sex, part of the world, have won our place for us. Ours is the task to ask what is general and accessible, suggestive beyond itself, in that range of particularity and parochial, private experience about which we have informed ourselves.

The answer to that question will emerge in the definition of those issues of general intelligibility to which, each in its own way, the new humanities also contribute. The key lies in asking one simple question: What does the private exemplify about what is shared and public? To what does the specific fact give testimony in what is shared? And how do we all exemplify a common experience of humanity? When we see the ways in which we are like, and the ways in which we are not like, the other or the rest, then we may speak intelligibly and claim a full and solemn hearing for ourselves. Then we serve scholarship as universities practice scholarship—that alone.

Acknowledgments

Chapter 1 was originally printed in Paul Ramsey and John F. Wilson, eds., *The Study of Religion in Colleges and Universities* (Princeton: Princeton University Press, 1970), pp. 159–89, and reprinted in my *Academic Study of Judaism, Essays and Reflections*, First Series (New York: KTAV Publishing House, 1975; repr. Chico: Scholars Press for Brown Judaic Studies, 1982), pp. 93–124.

Chapters 2 through 9 originally were presented at a conference on graduate education in Jewish learning held at Brown University on June 21–23, 1982, at the Center for the Study of Judaism (now: The Program in Judaic Studies) on a grant from the Max Richter Foundation of Rhode Island. I am grateful to the participants for revising their papers and permitting them to appear together in this book.

I take this occasion to reproduce the program of the original conference, so as to give all due credit to those who were kind enough to preside at the several sessions.

Philosophy   Monday, June 21, 1982

   Chair: Ernest Frerichs, Brown University
1. Jonathan Z. Smith, University of Chicago   Keynote
   Chair: Gary G. Porton, University of Illinois
2. Robert Alter, University of California, Berkeley   Literature
   Chair: Herbert H. Paper, Hebrew Union College
3. Baruch A. Levine, New York University   Semitics

Tuesday, June 22, 1982

   Chair: Wendell S. Dietrich, Brown University
4. Alexander Altmann, Brandeis University   Overview

Chair: Ivan G. Marcus, Jewish Theological
Seminary of America
5. Arnold J. Band, University of California, Los Literature
Angeles
Chair: Robert Freedman, Baltimore Hebrew
College
6. Marc Lee Raphael, Ohio State University History
Chair: David Goldenberg, Dropsie College
7. Calvin Goldscheider, Hebrew University Sociology

Wednesday, June 23, 1982

Chair: Moshe Goshen-Gottstein, Hebrew
University
8. Marvin Fox, Brandeis University Philosophy
Chair: William S. Green, University of Rochester
9. Jacob Neusner, Brown University Religious
Studies

Index

Agnon, S. Y., 83, 89, 92, 96, 104, 155
Agudat HaSoferim, 98
Akkadian, study of language in graduate programs, 108, 117–18
American Academy of Jewish Research, 179
Anti-Semitism in modern Jewish society, 67–68
Arabic, study of language in graduate programs, 108
Aramaic, study of language in graduate programs, 108–10, 112–13, 115–16, 119–20
Aristotle, 122, 124, 126, 130
Ashby, Philip, 17, 22
Assimilation and modern Jewish society, 70
Association for Jewish Studies, 106, 179–80
Auerbach, Erich, *Mimesis: The Representation of Reality in Western Literature*, 91

Babylonian Talmud, in Jewish studies, 10, 11, 13–14, 21
Baer, Fritz, 97
Balzac, Honoré de, 87, 91
Band, Arnold, 82
Bar-Ilan, Israel, 97
Baron, Devorah, 81
Baron, Salo, 97, 136
Beer Sheva University, 97
Bellah, Robert N., 43
Bergson, Henri, 123
Bialik, Hayyim Nahman, 86–88, 100–103
Bible, and commentary in Jewish studies, 11; Hebrew language and graduate study, 108; and Hebrew literature, 83–88, 93; and Jewish philosophy, 124, 128–29
Booth, Wayne, *The Rhetoric of Fiction*, 91–92
Bowman, Raymond, 116
Brandeis University, 97
Brenner, Y. H., 81
Brooks, Cleanth, *The Well Wrought Urn*, 91
Buber, Martin, 127–30
Buddhism, in study of comparative religions, 20

Christians, claims to be Jews, 9
Church and state, and religious studies, 40, 42
Cohen, Hermann, 123–24, 129
Cohn, Dorrit, *Transparent Minds*, 92
Columbia University, 7, 97
Comparative religions, study of, 39–40

Deshen, Shlomo, 115
Disciples, master-disciple relationship in graduate education, 46–61
Dissertations, rated in graduate studies, 34–39
Dropsie University, 158
Dubnow, Simon, 136
Dutch Reformed Church, and study of religions, 39
Dutch Universities Act, 39

Eliade, Mircea, 19, 24
Ethnicity, and modern Jewish society, 70–72

Fielding, Henry, 87

Fish, Stanley, 100
Fiske, Edward B., 173
Flaubert, Gustave, 92
Frankel, Yonah, 132

Geertz, Clifford, 43
Genette, Gérard, 92
Geiger, Abraham, 136
Germany, and religious studies, 50
Gilboa, Amir, 81
Glatzer, Nahum N., 11
Gnessin, Uri Nissan, 86, 92
Goldberg, Arthur J., 42
Goodenough, Erwin R., 17–18, 22
Graduate education: Israeli students, 157–61, 163; Jewish history, 135–49; Jewish philosophy, 121–34; programming of, 38–44, 54–61; social sciences and contemporary Jewish studies, 62–76
Graetz, Heinrich, 136
Greek, study of principles of rhetoric, 6
Green, William Scott, 177, 179
Greenberg, Uri Zvi, 86, 96

HaDoar, 97
Haifa University, 97
Halevi, Yehudah, 80, 85
Halkin, Hillel, 96–98
Hanagid, 80
Hassidism, in history of religions, 18–19; and Jewish history, 137
Hebrew language and literature in Jewish studies, 7–16, 106–20
Hebrew literature, and graduate education, 79–94, 108; modern Hebrew literature, 95–105, 108
Hebrew studies, language and literature, 5, 7
Hebrew Union College, 158
Hebrew University, 97
Hegel, Georg Wilhelm Friedrich, 127
Heiss, Ann, 142
Heschel, Abraham Joshua, 130
History: development of history of religions, 39; Jewish history and graduate studies, 135–49; Judaism in Jewish studies and history of religions, 7–25
Hrushovski, Benjamin, 98
HUCA, 97
Huizinga, Johan, 34
Humboldt, Wilhelm von, 60
Hurvitz, Avi, 119
Husserl, Hans-Georg 123

Indian religions, 51
Isaiah b. Amotz, 80
Islam: and Arabic religion, 51; in study of comparative religions, 20
Israel, graduate education, 157–61, 163

James, Henry, 91
Jewish history and graduate studies, 7–16, 135–49
Jewish learning and graduate studies, 33–61
Jewish philosophy and graduate education, 121–34
Jewish studies and social sciences, 62–76
Jewish Theological Seminary of America, 97, 158–63; and history of Judaism, 23
Johnson, Samuel, 90
Josephus, 136; works in Jewish learning, 12
Joyce, James, 80, 87; *Ulysses*, 80
JQR (*Jewish Quarterly Review*), 97
Judaic studies, components of, 7, 10–25
Judaism: 19, 21; centrality in modern society, 67–68; in general studies of religions, 43–44; graduate education, 46–61; history of in Jewish studies, 7–25; Jewish history in graduate studies, 136–37, 139; and Jewish philosophy, 121–34; philological discipline for study, 51; study in American Universities, 3–7, 9–16

Index

Kabbalah, in Jewish studies, 11, 20
Kalam, 124
Kant, Immanuel, 124
Kaplan, M. M., 130
Karaites, claims to be Jews, 9
Kaufmann, Yehezkel, *History of the Religion of Israel*, 24–25, 136
Kierkegaard, Søren, 127
Kitagawa, Joseph, 22–23
Klausner, Yosef, 88, 96, 99
Kraus, Karl, 96
Krochmal, Nachman Kohen, 136
Kurzweil, Baruch, 88, 96–98

Lahover, Yeruham Fishel, 88, 95
Languages: in graduate studies, 33; Hebrew, study of, 106–20; in study of Judaism, 5, 7, 16
Lardner, James, 172–73
Leavis, F. R., 99
Legal research in Jewish studies, 11
Literature: Hebrew literature in graduate education, 79–94; and Jewish philosophy, 124, 127, 129, 131–32; modern Hebrew literature, 95–105
Liturgy in Jewish studies, 11
Logic: in doctoral dissertations, 35; importance in Jewish studies, 13; and Jewish philosophy, 125–27
Lowenberg, Peter, 147
Lubbock, Percy, *The Craft of Fiction*, 91

Magical bowls, language of, 114–15
Mahler, Raphael, 136
Maimonides, Jewish philosophy, 123–26, 128–31
Manichaeism, in study of comparative religions, 20
Mann, Thomas, *Doktor Faustus*, 83
Mayakovsky, Vladimir, 80
Mendele (Sholem Yakob Abramovich), 93, 96
Messianic hope, and Jewish history, 137; in Jewish studies, 16, 18–19

Michener, James A., 59
Michigan Quarterly Review, 116
Middle East Institute at Harvard University, 7
Midrash: and Hebrew literature, 83–84, 87, 93; and Jewish philosophy, 128–29, 132
Miron, Dan, 98
Modernization of Jewish society and politics, 65–76
Moslem rationalism, philosophical traditions, 11
Moznayim, 97

Nabokov, Vladimir, 92
Near East languages and literature, study of, 5
Neusner, Jacob, 132, 137; *A History of the Jews in Babylonia*, 114
New Testament, in Jewish learning, 12
New York Times, 173
Noss, John, 41

Orlinsky, Harry, 119

Palestinian Talmud, in Jewish studies, 10–11, 13–14, 21
Paper, Herbert, 106
Parochial schools and Jewish studies, 4–10
Parsons, Talcott, 43
Perry, Menakhem, 86
Persian, study of language in graduate programs, 108, 112
Philo, 124, 129, 131; works in Jewish learning, 12
Philosophy, Jewish philosophy and graduate education, 121–34
Phoenician, study of language in graduate programs, 108
Plato, 122, 130
Polzin, Robert, 118
Prévost, Marcel, 91
Programming contemporary Jewish studies and social sciences, 62–76

Index

Protestantism: development of university study of religions, 51; graduate study of religions, 40–41, 43; in history of religions, 16–17
Publication of research material, 156
Public schools and religious studies, 41
Pushkin, Alexander, 88

Rabbinic Judaism: Hebrew language and graduate study, 107; and Jewish history, 136; study of, 3–4, 10–16
Reform Judaism, origin of beliefs, 6
Religion: church and state and religious studies, 40, 42; Judaism in history of religions, 16–25
Religious learning, study of Torah, 3–4, 7, 10–16
Religious studies, manner of study, 47–61; siting of programs, 38–44, 50–61
Research: in graduate studies, 34–39; publication of material, 156; social sciences and contemporary Jewish studies, 62–76
Rilke, Rainer Maria, 80
Roman Catholicism: development of university study of religions, 51; in history of religions, 16–17; and study of religions, 39, 41
Roman legal codification and Jewish studies, 6
Rosenzweig, Franz, 130
Rubin, Louis, 141
Russian Institute at Columbia University, 7

Saadia, 123–26
Sabbateans, claims to be Jews, 9, 18; and Jewish history, 137
Sadan, Dov, 88–89, 96–98
Sanskrit, and Indian religions, 51
Scholem, Gershom G., 17–18, 20, 22, 97
School District of Abington v. Schempp, 40
Schweid, Eli, 88

Science, place in Jewish studies, 11
Shaked, Gershon, 98
Shapira, Hayyim Nachman, 95
Smith, Jonathan Z., 47–48, 63, 65; structures of Judaism, 19, 21
Smith, Morton, 111
Soloveitchik, Joseph Dov, 130
Sonne, Avraham Ben Yitzhak, 83
Spinoza, Baruch, 48, 123
Stendhal (Marie Henri Beyle), 91
Sternberg, Meir, 86
Streng, Fred, 41

Tadmor, Hayim, 109
Talmud: and Hebrew literature, 83, 93; and Jewish philosophy, 128–29; in Jewish studies, 10–11, 13–14, 21, 51; language study in graduate programs, 109–10
Tarbiz, 97
Teaching contemporary Jewish studies, 73–76
Tel Aviv University, 97
Theses and doctoral dissertations discussed, 34–39
Thomas, Dylan, 80
Tochner, Meshullam, 89
Torah, study of, 3–5, 10–16
Troeltsch, Ernst, 14

UCLA, 97
Ugaritic, study of language in graduate programs, 108, 114
University of California at Berkeley, 97
University of Manchester, England, 39–40

Von Grunebaum, G. E. 27–28
Von Helmholtz, Hermann, 140

Washington Post, 172–73
Weber, Max, 14
Weinrich, Max, *A History of the Yiddish Language*, 112
Welch, Claude, *Graduate Education in Religion: A Critical Appraisal*, 40

Index 187

Wolff, Robert Paul, 141
Wolfson, Harry, 97
Woolf, Virginia, 92

Yeshiva University, 158

Yiddish, study of language in graduate programs, 112

Zion, 97
Zola, Émile, 91